PUBLIC RELATIONS FOR
HOSPITALITY MANAGERS

PUBLIC RELATIONS FOR HOSPITALITY MANAGERS
Communicating for Greater Profits

ALBERT E. KUDRLE

Public Relations/Communications Consultant

MELVIN SANDLER

University of New Hampshire

John Wiley & Sons, Inc.

New York • Chichester • Brisbane • Toronto • Singapore

This text is printed on acid-free paper.

Copyright © 1995 by John Wiley & Sons, Inc.

All rights reserved. Published simultaneously in Canada.

Reproduction or translation of any part of this work beyond
that permitted by Section 107 or 108 of the 1976 United
States Copyright Act without the permission of the copyright
owner is unlawful. Requests for permission or further
information should be addressed to the Permissions Department,
John Wiley & Sons, Inc., 605 Third Avenue, New York, NY
10158-0012.

This publication is designed to provide accurate and
authoritative information in regard to the subject
matter covered. It is sold with the understanding that
the publisher is not engaged in rendering legal, accounting,
or other professional services. If legal advice or other
expert assistance is required, the services of a competent
professional person should be sought.

Library of Congress Cataloging in Publication Data:
Kudrle, Albert E.
      Public relations for hospitality managers : communicating for
   greater profits / Albert E. Kudrle, Melvin Sandler.
         p.   cm.
      Includes index.
      ISBN 0-471-03977-2 (cloth : acid-free paper)
      1. Public relations—Hotels.   2. Public relations—Motels.
   3. Public relations—Restaurants.   I. Sandler, Mel.   II. Title.
   TX911.3.P77K83   1995
   659.2 '964794—dc20   94-45408
                                                            CIP

Printed in the United States of America

10   9   8   7   6   5   4   3   2   1

To Doris Kudrle, my ever-faithful wife, without whose encouragement, patience, and understanding this work could not have been completed.

Also to three public relations experts who taught me most of what I know about this craft: Frank Muni, William Scholz, and Peter Celliers.

—Albert Kudrle

To Matthew Sandler McLaughlin, age 6 months, who has demonstrated a quality public relations capability.

—Melvin Sandler

Foreword

Some 35 years ago, I entered my first graduate school class, heading for a Master's degree in public relations and communications. None of my friends, relatives, or fellow students knew then what public relations really was, how it affected them, and really what anyone with a degree in it might do to make a living. Certainly the hotel industry didn't have very much of a definition at that time either.

When I joined what was to become Sonesta Hotels back in 1961, the term "public relations" wasn't used in that organization. Somewhere between social hostess, guest relations, publicity, and promotion, the embryo was created that eventually developed into today's public relations function. This is a function that is carried on either internally (by the hotel or chain headquarters), externally (by outside public relations counsel), or both internally and externally (by both). What's interesting to me about its development as a true art form in the marketing mix is the plain fact that few hotels or chains execute the discipline with skill, with cost effectiveness, and with planned results in mind.

Most of us will have dabbled in public relations (a) through handling of a crisis when we or our employees just didn't know what to do, so we called our advertising agency, which recommended a PR professional; or (b) when we sent an announcement of an employee's promotion to a local paper or a hotel trade magazine; or (c) when we sponsored a Little League team that wears our logo or sent a check to the United Way in the hope that people will think we are good corporate citizens. I don't think that's real PR, nor do the authors of this book. Real public relations means just that. It means taking the time to manage your relations with the public as an entity that lives in their midst. It means managing the way the public thinks and feels about you so that they send you business and are happy to do so. It means managing a function that can be the most cost-effective part of the marketing mix—cheaper than advertising, sales, sales promotions, or research. In fact, public relations, properly planned and executed, has the highest return of all investments you can make to build business for your property or for your chain.

If this is the case, then why, you might ask, have so many invested so little and done it so poorly? Simply, the function is difficult to measure and it requires a commitment and belief that what your public thinks of you and your product is more important than just advertising the product. That's a very difficult concept for most owners and managers. Hence, hundreds of millions of dollars are spent (most of it uselessly) on creative advertising campaigns that are neither more measurable nor more productive. Other millions are spent turning over sales personnel while public relations is relegated to a third level, emerging only as a small piece of the total expenditure. While I do not wish to denigrate the need for either advertising or sales, PR rarely receives its share of the effort.

This book covers the basics in terms of the functional definition from media relations and PR campaigns, special events, and so on. The examples that are provided clearly exhibit what can be done and what can happen when it is done. My only reservation is that perhaps it does not go far enough in urging the reader to dramatically elevate the importance of the function itself. I'm not sure that my own experience is an example for all, but a review of the marketing accomplishments of five chains and hundreds of hotels nets the conclusion that public relations effectiveness was always a key to the success and very often the most important key. Nothing can be more important to the education of hotel managers now or in the future than to understand that PR can make a major difference in today's competitive marketplace. I would strongly urge those with outside PR counsel to read this book as well. The more you learn about public relations, the better. In the end, you will save expense and increase revenue, a combination that makes everyone very happy.

MICHAEL A. LEVEN

President and Chief Operating Officer
Holiday Inn Worldwide

Preface

As the manager of a smaller- to medium-sized hotel or restaurant, chances are you cannot afford a full-time public-relations person. Likewise, your budget won't allow you to retain the services of a public-relations agency.

Lacking professional counsel, training, and budget, you cannot expect to mount public-relations campaigns as comprehensive or sophisticated as those conducted by Fortune 500 corporations.

But with the guidance of this book, you can certainly learn how to develop public-relations/communications programs aimed at winning valuable media exposure. And it will also help you to communicate more effectively with your most important publics.

This book explains what public relations is, and, in addition, shows how, when properly practiced, a public-relations program can build business for deserving lodging and foodservice establishments.

One of the many important functions of a top public-relations executive of any major company is to interpret public attitudes toward policy and offer judgments on their effects on different publics *before* they are approved.

For this reason the manager who does not have the benefit of a professional public-relations director or counsel should read as extensively as possible in such fields as sociology (with the accent on social problems), public relations, employee relations, and community relations to keep abreast of current trends. An extensive Suggested References list appears at the end of this book.

You or someone you designate will be responsible for your establishment's public relations.

In some cases you will be competing with professionals in the public-relations field. Accordingly, you should be aware of the Code of Professional Standards for the Practice of Public Relations adopted by the Public Relations Society of America in 1988. The objective of this code is to "promote and maintain high standards of public service and ethical conduct" among the society's members. The code is reprinted in Appendix E. We recommend you read and adhere to its principles.

Acknowledgments

Most of the examples of successful public-relations campaigns or projects that appear throughout this book are reprinted from summaries of entries from the American Hotel & Motel Association's (AH&MA) Stars of the Industry Gold Key Public Relations Achievement Awards Program. These selected synopses were published in booklet format by the Association for distribution to interested members. Categories covered by this national AH&MA competition since 1989 include Community Service, Employee Relations, Guest Relations, and Special Events. Earlier competitions also focused on crisis public relations and media relations.

The authors are deeply indebted to AH&MA and Visa, corporate sponsor of the Stars of the Industry program since 1991, for permission to present these valuable case histories of imaginative public relations programs that produced eminently worthwhile results.

We also are sincerely appreciative of the significant contributions to this work of Beth Mignon, Director of Public Relations, and Thomas Hewitt, President, both of Hospitality Group, CHC, International (Carnival Hotels and Casinos). They provided us with valuable information for the text and graciously gave permission for use of a policy statement and excerpts from their "Public Relations Manual for Sales Managers."

In addition, we wish to thank the following people for their informative answers to our questions concerning the aims and functions of their PR programs:

Beth Shannon, Marketing Department
Red Roof Inns, Inc.

Alexandra Kent, Account Executive
The Gable Group
(public relations agency representing)
Forte Hotels, Inc.

Stephen P. Barba, President and Managing Partner
The Balsams Grand Resort Hotel
Dixville Notch, New Hampshire

Our sincere thanks, also, to Leslie Lefkowitz, director of public relations, The Ritz-Carlton, New York, for her invaluable assistance in reviewing sections of the manuscript and making a number of important suggestions.

In addition, we are deeply grateful to Sinthy Kounlasa for her proficiency, dedication, and perseverance in typing and assisting in assembling the manuscript.

Contents

PUBLIC RELATIONS FOR HOSPITALITY MANAGERS

1

What Public Relations Is and What It Can Do for You

A former travel editor and public-relations counsel for the Hyatt Corporation hotels, Peter Celliers, once said that "there are many misconceptions about public relations. One of the most widespread is that it's easy. And it is—it's as easy as painting the Sistine Ceiling if you're Michelangelo. Public relations can be as simple as a smile on the face of a room clerk or as complex as a bridge master's tournament. But in the final analysis, public relations is just targeted communications."[1]

Your establishment has public relations whether it recognizes it or not. Hotels and restaurants relate with numerous publics (groups of people). These may include

   —guests or customers
   —employees
   —community opinion leaders and other residents
   —the traveling public, business and leisure travelers who
     are potential guests or customers
   —the general public
   —the media

—suppliers

—other segments of the travel or food-service industries (travel agents and restaurant guide publishers, for example)

—shareholders, if your hotel or restaurant is owned or operated by a publicly held corporation

—corporate officers (same as above).

Public relations should be part of an overall marketing communications program. The program at an independent property encompasses only that hotel or restaurant. If the establishment belongs to a system, its efforts must dovetail with the organization's overall corporate communications.

In either case, such a program might consist of

- public relations,
- advertising,
- internal communications, and
- sales promotion.

Public relations has been called an oft-misunderstood calling, craft, or process. Thus it may be helpful at the outset to examine what public relations is and is not.

Some otherwise knowledgeable hospitality executives frequently confuse public relations with publicity—one of its tools. Still others see no difference between public relations and advertising. Chapter 4 goes into detail about what separates advertising from public relations.

To clear up any misconceptions, perhaps it would be most useful to start by setting forth what public relations is not.

First, public relations is not a cure-all for the ills and problems that confront hotels, restaurants, and their executives.

One of the most common misunderstandings of public relations is that it is a kind of black magic that will make people think favorably of a hospitality organization whether such opinions are deserved or not. Nothing could be further from the truth.

Specifically, though, having the name of your hotel or restaurant mentioned in the print media or on radio or television is publicity, not public relations. Publicity is a vital part of public relations and also one of its most important tools, as mentioned earlier. This is because securing unpaid editorial space or time in the media is a fundamental goal of most public-relations programs. In Chapter 3 we will discuss this more thoroughly.

Also, public relations is not sales promotion, point-of-sale displays, contests, speeches, personal appearances, or membership in organizations. Rather, public relations includes all of these, but is "larger than the sum of its parts."

Now that we have examined what public relations is not, let's explore what it really is.

There probably are as many ways to define public relations as there have been people who have tried to define it. The simplest is this: Public relations is doing the right thing and getting credit for it. Another equally valid way to describe public relations is that it is the planned effort to influence opinion through acceptable performance and two-way communication.

Public relations is frequently abbreviated as PR. Thus it has been said that it can also be reduced to this simple formula:

P for performance plus **R** for recognition equals **PR**.

Public relations is the total communications effort of a person, a company, an agency, a group, a government, or any organization to its various publics.[2]

The *Dictionary of Advertising Terms* defines public relations as (1) activities of persons or organizations intended to promote understanding of and good will toward themselves or their products or services, (2) the degree to which such entities have obtained understanding and good will from their publics, and (3) a management staff function that seeks to assess and favorably influence public opinion of a person, good, or organization by delivering messages to such publics without incurring direct media costs.

A chapter in a book by Edward L. Bernays about public relations has as its title—and defines its subject as—"The Engineering of Consent."

> Much negative reaction to public relations was engendered by pioneer public relations expert Edward Bernays' description of the theory and practice of public relations as the "engineering of consent." Taken out of context, this characterized public relations as a form of manipulation of people's minds. Nothing was further from Bernays' intent. He viewed public relations as a profession, and he submitted that its activities should be planned and executed in line with scientific principles, using the dispassionate approach and methods similar to those of the engineering profession.
>
> In short, his way was to define the objectives, to bring all available resources to bear upon the problem and to initiate action designed to improve the situation and then to review the results critically.[3]

Chances are most public-relations practitioners would agree that PR is what the public perceives. In other words, it is the sum total of what the public sees, reads, hears, and feels. What the public perceives may be accurate or not. All too often it is not. When this happens it is generally because public relations has not been controlled—the proper message has not been sent to the proper publics. The job of PR is to recognize that fact and take advantage of it.

John W. Hill, founder of Hill & Knowlton, the world's largest public-relations firm, has this to say about defining public relations:

> Unlike law or medicine, public relations cannot be defined in precise terms. The term has been brought into use to cover a mul-

titude of activities, many of which are wholly unrelated. A Washington lobbyist or "influence peddler," a specialist in getting names mentioned in society or gossip columns; a night club press agent, and dozens of others all may have a shingle on their doors reading "public relations," as they have a perfect right to do if they want it.[4]

Two other public relations practitioners put it this way:

> When a customer deals with any member of your organization and is satisfied, that is good public relations. When your appearance and knowledge make a favorable impression on anyone in your community or in your industry or in the media, that is good public relations.
> When you contribute your time and effort to a worthy cause, that is good public relations. In short any contact you have with another human being is part of public relations, your personal total communications effort.

Philip Lesly, a leading public relations counselor, offers several definitions of PR:

> public relations can be defined as helping an organization and its publics accommodate to each other.
> public relations, the science that deals with the person's opinions and with the relationship of an organization with the people it involves.
> as a means of interchanging attitudes . . . .
> as the discipline that deals with public attitudes . . . .
> Perhaps the most important force affecting all organizations . . . today is the opinion of people. Businessmen realize this when they talk of "good will." . . .
> management executives today realize that along with production, sales, accounting, finance, engineering, their businesses must have the most expert assistance in developing and maintaining good will—or "public relations" as it is most commonly called.
> At its best, public relations is a bridge to change. It is a means to adjust to new attitudes that have been caused by change. It is a means of stimulating attitudes in order to create changes.[5]

WHAT PUBLIC RELATIONS CAN AND CANNOT DO

Skeptical hospitality executives may ask: "Why should I be interested in PR?" In other words, "What's in it for me?"

One objective of any public-relations program should be to determine what your establishment is, how good it is, and what distinguishes it from the pack in terms of your customers' needs, and then communicate it so that the public perceives it properly. This is called "positioning." Obtaining the answers to these questions and getting this information to the proper publics will help you avoid falling into the trap best described in the following: If you don't know where you're going, any road will do.

Other equally important objectives that should be considered in developing any PR program include improving sales, lifting profits, letting the community know more about the hotel or restaurant, indicating the advantages it offers guests or patrons as compared with its competitors, and building a good relationship with the media. Chapter 5 describes how to achieve the latter.

Properly planned, a public-relations program can call widespread attention to the achievements of the hotel or restaurant represented or the benefits of using the product or idea being promoted.

Denver's independent Brown Palace Hotel, for example, celebrated 100 years of continuous operation with a year-long public-relations program. Entitled "100 Years of Memories," the carefully planned campaign kicked off with a news conference on the hotel's 99th anniversary. During the next 12 months, the Brown Palace offered many programs to highlight its centennial celebration. These events included historic tours of the hotel twice a week and displays of antique artifacts including old china, menus, guest registers, and other memorabilia, some of it from the hotel's collection and some donated by former guests. The hotel's restaurants promoted a number of menu items from the past, offering recipes to guests. New ones were also created in honor of the 100th anniversary.

During the anniversary year numerous special room packages were developed for guests. A commemorative edition of "The Brown Palace Story," a history of the hotel, was also published. Price of admission to a "birthday" party open to the public was a toy donated to a local children's home. Another party was held for present and former employees. "The '100 Years of Memories' was a tremendous success for the Brown Palace. It made more people aware of the hotel through media stories or visits to the property, and increased revenue for the hotel during the year."[6]

As mentioned earlier, one way to define public relations is doing the *right thing* and getting credit for it. It is important to remember, therefore, that public relations cannot make a bad institution, product, or idea good. As public-relations pioneer John W. Hill puts it, "Public relations has no power to create any lasting value where none exists."

A business can prosper and grow only with the understanding and support of public opinion. To achieve this is one of the main objectives of public relations.

Thus management's attitudes, policies, and actions must merit public regard. The property also must be in good physical condition. Only then can you take advantage of the next step, getting credit for doing the right thing. This is accomplished via communications, which has been called the working tool of public relations. PR admittedly can't make a bad situation good. But it can make a good story better and a bad story not so bad.

Let's say a restaurant employee saves a young person's life by performing the Heimlich maneuver (a maneuver used to dislodge food from the windpipe). Preventing the child from choking on a bit of food makes a good story. An alert manager should quickly provide the news media with the full name, age, address, job title, and employment history of the employee. Providing this information and, possibly, adding a few well-chosen words of praise regarding the hero or heroine can easily make the "good story better."

Conversely, if executives of the hotel or restaurant have built up a reputation in the community or with the media for dependability and truthfulness, a "bad story" can sometimes be made "not so bad." Should a fire occur in a restaurant kitchen, for instance, or a suicide in a hotel, the resulting news story may omit or "bury" the name of the establishment rather than feature it in the headline or opening paragraph of the article.

Another long-range objective of any PR campaign is to help project a favorable image of your hotel or restaurant. Public-relations people talk a great deal about the image of an organization and how to go about improving it.

An image has been defined as a popular conception of a person or institution projected especially through the mass media. But it is worth noting that an equally valid definition of an image is exact likeness or the optical counterpart of an object produced by an optical device (as a lens or mirror) or an electronic device.

Thus the owner of a hotel or restaurant that is poorly managed or badly in need of repairs cannot hope to have the tarnished image of the establishment burnished simply by phoning a news tip to the media or calling a news conference. To correct the situation, the quality of the product or the service being offered must first be improved. What needs to be done is to determine, insofar as image is concerned, where you are, where you want to be, and how you can best get there.

The public relations person, in the view of one expert in the field, is not a magician who will whitewash a spotted image. Nor is he or she a good-natured buffer who'll keep inquisitive reporters at arm's length when management does not wish to discuss an unpleasant subject. Instead, the public-relations practitioner has been described as a catalyst. Acting on his or her suggestion, management should take action to obtain as favorable a consensus—concerning the property or its operators—as is reasonable.

NOTES

1. Celliers, Peter J. "Setting Public Relations Targets." Remarks delivered at the 1977 Discover America National Conference and Travel Mart.
2. Culligan, Matthew J., and Green, Dolph. *Getting Back to the Basics of Public Relations and Publicity.* Crown Publishers, New York, 1982.
3. Budd, John F., Jr. *An Executive's Primer on Public Relations.* Chilton Book Co., Philadelphia, PA, 1969. (Source for Bernays' description of public relations: Bernays, Edward L. *Public Relations.* University of Oklahoma Press, Norman, OK, 1952, Chapter 14, The Engineering of Consent.)
4. Hill, John W. *The Making of a Public Relations Man.* NTC Business Books, David McKay Co., Lincolnwood, IL, 1963.
5. Lesly, Philip (editor). *Lesly's Public Relations Handbook,* 2nd ed. Prentice-Hall, Englewood Cliffs, NJ, 1978.
6. American Hotel & Motel Association, Stars of the Industry Gold Key Public Relations Achievement Awards, Special Events—One-time Only—Individual Property Winner—The Brown Palace Hotel, Denver, CO, 1993.

2

PR as a Strategy in the Marketing Plan

As publicity is a tool of public relations, so public relations is a tool of marketing.

Most hotel and restaurant systems therefore foster a close relationship between public relations and marketing. In many cases the director of public relations reports to the vice president of marketing or other chief marketing officer.

Even if the top public-relations person in such an organization reports directly to the president or CEO, marketing and PR people closely coordinate their plans and programs. It is up to the independent hotel manager or restaurant owner to make sure there is this same close relationship between public relations and marketing in his or her property. What's the reason behind this strategy?

Chapter 1 suggests that public relations should be part of the overall marketing communications program. In recent years this idea has been expanded, and now public relations generally is considered an essential link in the marketing chain. In other words, public relations should be one of the strategies aimed at making your marketing plan successful.

Marketing has been defined as

> the business task of: (1) selecting attractive target markets;
> (2) designing customer-oriented products and services; and (3) de-
> veloping effective distribution and communication programs with
> the aim of producing high consumer purchase and satisfaction and
> high company attainment of its objectives.[1]

Michael Leven, president and COO of Holiday Inn
Worldwide, has long been widely acknowledged as one of the
lodging industry's leading marketing executives. While serving
as president of Days Inns, he came up with a succinct definition of marketing in response to a question concerning the difference between sales and marketing. He put it this way:
"Sales is getting rid of things and marketing is deciding what
to get rid of."

Public relations was defined in 1975 by 65 public relations
leaders as

> a distinctive management function which helps establish and
> maintain mutual lines of communication, understanding, accep-
> tance and cooperation between an organization and its publics; in-
> volves the management of problems or issues; helps management
> keep informed on and responsive to public opinion; defines and
> emphasizes the responsibility of management to serve the public
> interest; helps management keep abreast of and effectively utilize
> change, serving as an early warning system to help anticipate
> trends; and uses research and sound and ethical communications
> techniques as its principal tools.[2]

A number of newer terms have been developed as substitutes for public relations, some of which include the word
marketing, indicating the close relationship between these two
functions. Some of the terms are marketing communications,
marketing public relations, corporate public relations, relationship marketing, and megamarketing.

Let's examine each of these closely.

A leading educator in the marketing field, Philip Kotler, S. C.

Johnson & Son Distinguished Professor of International Marketing, J. I. Kellogg Graduate School of Management, Northwestern University, defines marketing as

> the strategically coordinated application of economic, psychological, political, and public relations skills to gain the cooperation of a number of parties in order to enter and/or operate in a given market.[3]

Here's a brief explanation of relationship marketing, also a relatively new term:

- Relationship marketing strategies are concerned with a broader scope of external "market" relationships, which include suppliers, business referral and "influence" sources.
- Relationship marketing also focuses on the internal (staff) relationships critical to the success of (external) marketing plans. "Internal marketing" aims to achieve continuous improvement in marketing performance.
- Improving marketing performance ultimately requires a resolution (or realignment) of the competing interests of customers, staff and shareholders, by changing the way managers "manage" the activities of the business.[4]

Corporate public relations include activities such as media relations, government relations, community relations, employee communications, and general public affairs and is often viewed as an activity that is somewhat unrelated to the marketing tasks of selling a product or service. Experience shows that corporate public relations is essential in providing the linkages to achieve a positive reputation about the product or service. Examples in which corporate communications might be critical are the company's standing with the community at large in circumstances of a disaster or crisis, governmental agencies where zoning or parking spaces are at stake, educational institutions that provide future employees, etc. In essence, your standing in community, state, or national circles has significant impact on the strategy that has been established to sell a product or service.

Subsequent chapters on community and employee relations and others throughout this book will explain how public relations and its related activities lay the groundwork for the ultimate sales of product or service and for pleasing patrons to the point where they become repeat customers.

This brings us to the topic of marketing public relations (MPR). Thomas L. Harris, in his comprehensive book *The Marketer's Guide to Public Relations: How Today's Top Companies Are Using the New PR to Gain a Competitive Edge,* defines MPR as

> the process of planning, executing and evaluating programs that encourage purchase and consumer satisfaction through credible communication of information and impressions that identify companies and their products with the needs, wants, concerns and interests of consumers.[5]

These newer terms and definitions are outlined to suggest that industry professionals employ a variety of methods to try to obtain and retain customers. Advertising obviously is still an effective method to reach out to potential customers.

But competing messages frequently saturate radio, TV networks, and printed matter, to the point where product identification can be so glamorized that message recognition becomes blurred. The wide selection of excellent competitive products and services on the market offer the customer many choices but few criteria by which to select.

Public relations and marketing public relations attempt to reach these overloaded message boards by using news/broadcast-type opportunities. Philip Kotler suggests that "PR has come into this (marketing) mix because it is much more cost effective. We now think we can get more impact through events, event marketing and news making, and, in general, there's more credibility.[6]

Thomas L. Harris says:

> The explosive growth of marketing public relations has been fueled by the simultaneous recognition of its intrinsic value by

leading marketers and the ability of the marketing public relations professional to devise programs that support marketing strategies precisely and cost effectively. In its marketing support function, public relations is used to achieve a number of objectives. The most important of these are to raise awareness, to inform and educate, to gain understanding, to build trust, to make friends, to give people reasons (and in some cases permission) to buy and finally to create a climate of consumer acceptance.[7]

The topic of this chapter, "PR as a Strategy in the Marketing Plan," emphasizes the integration of the many approaches to achieve the goal of obtaining and retaining customers. In fact, this is the focus of this book. When management communicates effectively with its three major publics, guests, employees, and community opinion leaders and residents, it is well on the road to developing a productive marketing plan. Should an emergency occur and be handled competently, according to plan, that's the icing on the cake.

A survey of 100 marketing company executives showed integration of advertising, promotion, public relations, and all other forms of marketing communications was the consensus winner as the most important factor influencing how strategies will be set in the next three to five years. These study results were presented at the Promotion Marketing Association of America's national conference in March 1993.

At this meeting, Larry Light, the former chairman and CEO of the international division of Backer Spielvogel Bates Worldwide said, "The reason integrated marketing is important is consumers integrate your messages whether you like it or not. The messages cannot be kept separate. Integrated marketing is not an option. I don't agree with those who say it's time you got on the integrated marketing bandwagon. All marketing is integrated in the mind of the consumer. Your only choice is how that message is integrated."[8]

Hilton International is reported to use the term marketing communications instead of public relations and defines it as "the process by which we create a positive image and customer preference through third-party endorsements."[9] Also, advertising and other promotional techniques can build on this platform of a positive image. The encouragement of customer recommendations, employee support, positive media recognition, and community support will create the desired image and thus result in attracting more business.

Harris suggests many uses of marketing public relations:[10*]

- to position companies as leaders and experts
- to build consumer confidence and trust
- to introduce new products
- to revitalize, relaunch, and reposition mature products
- to communicate new benefits of old products
- to promote new uses for old products
- to involve people with products
- to build or maintain interest to a product category
- to cultivate new markets
- to reach secondary markets
- to reinforce weak markets
- to extend the reach of advertising
- to counteract consumer resistance to advertising
- to break through commercial clutter
- to make news before advertising
- to make advertising noteworthy
- to complement advertising by reinforcing messages and legitimizing claims
- to supplement advertising by communicating other product benefits
- to tell the product story in greater depth
- to increase viewership of sponsored television programs
- to influence opinion leaders
- to gain awareness through other than advertising media
- to test marketing concepts
- to reinforce sales promotion campaigns
- to reach demographically defined markets
- to reach psychographically defined markets
- to identify companies and products with ethnic markets
- to tailor marketing programs to local audiences
- to raise brand awareness through title sponsorships
- to distinguish companies and their products from the competition

- to create new media and new ways to reach consumers
- to win consumer support by identifying companies and brands with causes they care about
- to interpret the impact of emerging issues on the marketplace
- to open communication channels between marketers and groups who could negatively impact achievement of marketing goals
- to communicate marketing decisions in the public interest
- to defend products at risk
- to gain distribution
- to build store traffic
- to generate sales inquiries
- to motivate the sales force
- to win retailer support.

Many of the above suggested applications of MPR can be illustrated by the following widely known activities and programs:

- McDonald's support and sponsorship of the Ronald McDonald facilities for families obtaining medical treatment for their children;
- Anheuser-Busch's use of the Clydesdales in tours and community activities;
- the sponsorship of marathons, bikeathons, etc. for good causes such as March of Dimes and multiple sclerosis;
- the Pillsbury Bake-off contest, which has been held since 1949;
- Rockport Shoe Company's development of walking exercise programs with the endorsement of the American Podiatric Medical Association;
- the introduction of the Ford Taurus a year before its availability via shows and press activities;
- the introduction of the NeXT computer by Steve Jobs, one of the inventors of the Apple Computer, after an extended absence from the computer industry;
- the opening of a McDonald's in Moscow;
- Johnson & Johnson's handling of the Tylenol crisis with an open discussion of the issue, making executives

available to the press, TV, and radio as well as public officials;

- Pizza Hut's program to encourage reading via a recognition and reward program in schools;
- Anheuser-Busch's responsible drinking programs;
- the March Across America sponsored by Tang for MADD (Mothers Against Drunk Driving).

For many hotel executives who have tried it, the primary function of their public-relations programs has been marketing support to sell rooms and food.

The chief executive of a widely known, medium-size resort hotel (232 rooms) points to a number of successful marketing activities supported by public-relations efforts. He is Stephen P. Barba, president and managing partner, The Balsams Grand Resort Hotel, Dixville Notch, New Hampshire.

When Barba took over The Balsams in 1966, the physical plant was run down, it lacked adequate furniture and furnishings, and business had fallen to a low ebb. Less than two decades later, as a result of an enlightened management, an infusion of capital, and application of sophisticated technology, the resort had earned a four-star rating with the Mobil Travel Guide and four diamonds from AAA.

In Stephen Barba's view, it is not enough for a marketing program simply to produce a product and, with the help of public relations, to announce it to the world. Instead, he feels, to be successful, public relations must change people's behavior.

In today's highly mobile society, people are constantly on the move, changing jobs and marriage partners, moving to new locations, etc. Similarly, many people look for a new vacation destination every year.

Before coming to The Balsams, most guests had "sampled" a number of other resort hotels; however, once they stay at The Balsams, "most come back again and again, having found something stable and constant in their lives," Barba says. This applies not only to older guests but to families with young children.

Of the thousands of guests who stay at The Balsams every year, 83 percent are returning after a previous visit, according to Barba. A recent statistically comprehensive survey of 7,000 former Balsams guests clearly documents the "outstanding reputation" the hotel enjoys among its guests.

This has come about because the resort hotel does everything possible to establish a personal relationship with all guests, from the moment they arrive. They see their names prominently posted in the lobby on a list of guests arriving that day. While staying at the hotel they have the same table in the dining room every day and the same wait staff, and their guest room is cleaned by the same housekeeper throughout their stay. This gives them a chance to develop a relationship with these staff members. In making reservations, many guests will ask for the same dining room table and the same room they had the previous year, so that they can be sure of being served by the staff members with whom they are acquainted. Once they leave, guests get personalized letters from the hotel twice a year, and a guest newsletter to remind them that they are part of the Balsams "family."

Management recognizes the importance of the strong ties they have established with former guests—or are working to build with first-time guests. Accordingly, the hotel strongly markets to its past guests.

Advertising materials, including brochures and videos, are designed in cooperation with the hotel's PR consultant to encourage guests to show these to business associates, friends, neighbors, and relatives to recommend that they try The Balsams. In effect, the hotel depends, in part, on former guests to act as salespeople for the property. As a result, "The great majority of first-time guests [come] . . . because they have heard about us from [former guests] . . . . Viewers of our video brochure, on average, show the tape in their homes to seven people outside their own family," Barba says.

To further cultivate returning guests each receives a present—a pint of maple syrup with a hand-written label. Those returning for the 10th year get another gift—a hand-thrown, hand-painted vase. Every 20-year guest receives a matted and framed antique picture of The Balsams, inscribed "In appreciation of two decades of mutual esteem."

Recognizing the potential to attract more guests to this destination resort in a remote area close to New Hampshire's Canadian border, Barba retained the services of a public-relations firm in 1985.

An early business analysis revealed that Sunday night occupancy was consistently lower than on any other night of the week. Guests tended to depart in great numbers on Sundays, but most check-ins did not occur until Mondays. This was largely attributed to length of stay and work week schedules.

How to compensate for this drop off in guest arrivals? The answer was the Sunday Night Special—an attractive rate offered to those living only a short distance from the hotel or those on vacation in the area, but not staying at The Balsams. A combination advertising and public-relations program was developed to reach this audience. News releases were sent to local newspapers and radio stations; ads were placed in the same near market media. Direct mail advertising to nearby residents and former guests living in the area used the theme "get to know your neighbors." Letters also were sent to area groups. As a result, within a year a significant increase in Sunday night occupancy had been achieved, according to Barba. He said Sunday Night Special guests now account for about 10 percent of the Sunday night house count.

Following the success of the Sunday Night Special program, the same offer was extended to Canadian residents living not too far from the hotel. Called "Club Canada," it offers those eligible a preferred rate on days and under conditions favorable to the hotel. It was advertised and publicized in much the same way as the Sunday Night Special, with worthwhile results.

A further extension of the same concept, called the "Notch Club," offers "membership" to anyone who has taken advantage of a Sunday Night Special. Members may stay at the hotel at a reduced rate on any night of the week on a space-available basis. Management attributes incremental year-round occupancy increases to this program.

Spring is traditionally convention time at The Balsams. But several years ago attendance at these meetings declined severely, owing to depressed business conditions. The depressed economy caused several groups that regularly met at the hotel to cancel or not to book their spring meetings. Golf was one of the favorite spring recreational activities of members of these organizations.

In an effort to replace this lost business, a golf special rate and offer was developed, advertised, and promoted through news releases and other media contacts. The results of this short-term combined marketing/public-relations program were "most rewarding," Barba said.

Use of this program continues to help sell rooms during spring and fall periods when conventions do not fill the hotel. (The Balsams does not accept meeting business during the summer social season.) More golf special guests came to the hotel during the spring and fall convention seasons in 1994, for example, than in the previous year.

Barba contends that in his discussions with other resort executives all over the country, he has discovered only one other property that has established close ties with its guests. Most resorts, he says, try only to make sure that the guest experience is an enjoyable one.

The hotel's mission statement emphasizes that it is management's intention to do business with returning guests, and its marketing/public-relations efforts are aimed at accomplishing this objective.

Not only has the combined marketing/public-relations program at the hotel been successful, as documented above, but Barba points out that "we have reduced our paid advertising expenses and, nevertheless, increased the public's appreciation for The Balsams."

Ronald H. Nykiel is a former marketing executive in the Marriott and Stouffer organizations. Currently a hospitality educator, he teaches marketing at the Conrad N. Hilton College of Hotel and Restaurant Management at the University of Houston. Nykiel has a deep appreciation for the value of public relations in the marketing process.

A firm believer in the importance of setting goals and then getting organized—step-by-step—to achieve them, he outlined his views on public relations in a 1989 book on hospitality marketing as follows:

HOW PUBLIC RELATIONS CAN BE APPLIED

Once the objectives for your public relations plan have been established and tied into the overall marketing plan, it is time to consider how to apply or execute those ideas. You must first answer some questions:

1. What medium can best execute this strategy?
2. Who are the key contacts for this task?
3. Is it necessary to establish or resolidify any personal relationships before executing the strategy?
4. Is our approach carefully thought out? What are the potential downside risks?
5. Do we have a delivery package ready for the media?

The delivery package is essential and should contain any required copy, plots, key contacts, phone numbers, and so on. Although there is no guarantee your copy or materials will be used, it is much more likely that your public-relations message will correspond to your intentions if you make a delivery package available. The following list will aid you in compiling a package that will be useful to the media.

These six recognition factors will only bring you to the door. Now you will need some guidelines for answering questions, which will eventually allow you to turn the lock of the door and enter. The keys that follow are not all-inclusive, nor are they original, but they are very practical.

KEY 1: TELL THE TRUTH

The message you want to convey should be pure fact. The media want credible, straightforward, and truthful material and relationships. This simply means your materials should be thorough and honest. It does not mean you need to reveal every detail, confidential data, or private source, nor does it mean you should violate confidentialities.

KEY 2: BE RESPONSIVE

You may not provide nor have all the answers at your fingertips for every question or inquiry. Do not lie; say, "It's not available," or "I can't comment on that," or "I do not have that information with me; however, I will call you and provide it today." Then get the information fast and provide it accurately.

KEY 3: PROVIDE THE FACTS AND FOLLOW UP

Supply the key facts and provide them in print or a handout to lessen the chance of being misquoted on key data. If at all possible, follow up and seek to go over the facts or key numbers for accuracy. If you do not have a requested statistic, get it and follow up with a phone call and/or note to be sure the accurate numbers reach the media.

KEY 4: BE CONCISE

People usually get into trouble with the media for what they say, not what they do not say. Provide the facts in a concise, uneditorialized, and unexaggerated manner. By all means, be precise and accurate. Ranges may be okay, but pulling the numbers out of the blue sky is a disaster.

KEY 5: BUILD THE RELATIONSHIP

If you follow steps 1 through 4 by being truthful, responsible, factual, and concise, you are on your way to achieving the fifth practical key—building a good relationship. Hostile attitudes, reactionary statements to sensitive questions, aloofness, or a combative position destroys relations and may result in very negative reactions. Work hard at being in control of yourself and your responses, no matter what you think of the media, interviewer, or individuals with whom you deal in these relationships. After all, an enemy or someone who dislikes you is not going to give you space or air time.

PUBLIC RELATIONS AND THE PRESS
Recognition Factors

1. *Identify your purpose.* What is your purpose or reason for seeking the public relations exposure? If your purpose is to make others aware of your new restaurant theme, be sure that is exactly what you convey—don't let it be lost in a story about your chef's auto collection. Be precise and be sure your intent is communicated.

2. *Identify your target.* Who is your target? Is it prospective consumers of your product? Is it the local financial community? Is it recognition of one of your employees, thus employees' morale? Is it food sales, beverage sales, room sales, brand awareness? Think it out and identify how and where in the media you will best achieve your objectives.

3. *Understand the other perspective.* You know your purpose and you now know your target. That is your perspective. What is the press's interest? Identify and understand their interests. Determine how you can place your purpose and target within a package that directly meets the interest of the press or other media. To be successful here, think about what will help their circulation, listening audience, etc.

4. *Tailor your preparation.* Having identified your purpose, your target, and the media's perspective, tailor your preparation to include all three. Be sure to include everything that the press will need to convey the story—photos, names, releases. Be sure it's typed, double-spaced, and in the style the medium is currently utilizing. Follow the editorial style of your selected medium at all times.

5. *Know the transmission channels.* Knowing where to send your material means knowing the difference between a news and a feature story. News should be directed to the (newspaper's) city desk; feature stories should go to the appropriate editor, such as the entertainment editor or the restaurant editor. Better yet, get

to know the editors who can be of most help to you and culti-vate the relationship, but don't wear it out.

6. *The human elements.* People do not like extra work or being pres-sured, and most cannot afford the time to tell you the ground rules. People are basically lazy. This sounds cruel, but it should help you understand how to deal with the human element. Find out the deadlines in advance. Do not waste your time or the valuable time of media contacts. Do as much of their work as you can. Remember, if it is well prepared and you do most of the work for them, your material may be used. If you do not do the work, you can expect nothing to appear. Also remember to be available for immediate response to any questions or clarifica-tions the media may have on your story. If you are unavailable, your material may be scrapped or come out wrong.

Delivery Package Requirements

Addresses and phone numbers of key media contacts
Addresses and phone numbers of key corporation personnel
Approval procedures and required forms
Biographies of key personnel
Briefing sheets on individuals, company, product, etc.
Brochures, if applicable
Cancellation procedures and policy
"Canned" formats, releases, letterheads, logos, symbols, etc.
Confidentiality statements/procedures
Contacts list and phone numbers/procedures
Copy samples and actual copy
Displays, podiums with logos, etc.
News conference procedures list
One person to call and his or her phone number (usually public
     relations contact)
Photo inventory of products, people, etc.
Photo library and selection ready for press
Previous problems files and checklist
Previous questions files and checklist
Price/rate information
Procedures for distribution
Promotion package on firm or product
Request forms—data, photo, product information, etc.
Scrapbook or clipping files
Speech copies for distribution.[11]

NOTES

 1. Kotler, Philip. "Public Relations vs. Marketing: Dividing the Conceptual Domain and Operational Turf." Position Paper Prepared for the Public Relations Colloquium, San Diego, January 24, 1989.
 2. Cutlip, Scott M., Center, Allen II, and Broom, Glen M. *Effective Public Relations,* 6th ed., p. 4. Prentice-Hall, Englewood Cliffs, NJ, 1985.
 3. Kotler, Philip. "Megamarketing." *Harvard Business Review,* March–April 1986.
 4. Christopher, Martin, Payne, Adrian, and Ballantyne, David. *Relationship Marketing: Bringing Quality, Customer Service and Marketing Together.* Butterworth Heinemann Reed International Books, Stoneham, MA, 1991.
 5. Harris, Thomas L. *The Marketer's Guide to Public Relations: How Today's Top Companies Are Using the New P.R. To Gain a Competitive Edge.* John Wiley, New York, 1991. Copyright © 1991 by John Wiley & Sons. Reprinted by permission.
 6. "Kotler Foresees Integrated Future." *Business Marketing,* September 1993, p. 35.
 7. Harris, Thomas L. "How MPR Adds Value to Integrated Marketing Communications." *Public Relations Quarterly,* Summer 1993.
 8. "Integrated Marketing: Who's In Charge Here?" *Advertising Age,* March 22, 1993, p. 3.
 9. Miller, Jessica. "Marketing Communications." *The Cornell HRA Quarterly,* October 1993, pp. 48–53.
10. Harris, Thomas L. *The Marketer's Guide to Public Relations: How Today's Top Companies Are Using the New P.R. to Gain a Competitive Edge.* John Wiley, New York, 1991. Copyright © 1991 by John Wiley & Sons. Reprinted by permission.
11. Nykiel, Ronald A. *Marketing in the Hospitality Industry,* 2nd ed., Van Nostrand Reinhold, New York, 1989. Reprinted by permission.

3

Establishing and Maintaining Effective Media Relations

Publicity has been called the tip of the public-relations iceberg. Effective media relations generates publicity. Consequently, media relations is one of the most important phases of the public relations process. This is because it is in the media that the most tangible and visible results of your public-relations program—publicity—may occur.

Webster's defines publicity as "an act or device designed to attract public interest; specif: information with news value issued as a means of gaining public attention or support." The same source also defines medium (the singular of media) as, among other things, "a means of effecting or conveying something" and "a channel of communication; a publication or broadcast that carries advertising or a mode of artistic expression or communication."[1]

Unfortunately, since publicity is so easy to see, far too many business executives seem to hold the opinion that publicity is synonymous with public relations. As pointed out in Chapter 1, public relations has many other important aspects in addition to publicity.

Hotels, resorts, motor inns, and restaurants need favorable publicity to project the proper image to the various publics or audiences they serve or would like to serve. They also would like their messages to be received by those individuals or groups on whom they depend to recommend business, to provide proper service to guests and patrons, and to provide supplies and equipment of the desired quality. They must communicate effectively with these people if they are to succeed.

The publics they strive to reach through the media include former guests, prospective guests, travel agents, meeting and convention planners, business travel managers, community leaders, local or area residents, tour operators, taxi drivers, toll takers at nearby toll highway interchanges, employees, potential employees, and suppliers. Publicity in the right media conveys a message to the people—publics—you want to reach.

Thus one of the first tasks in developing effective media relations is to identify your target media. The news media can be classified by the audiences they reach and the means they employ to carry their messages. Most people in the United States get their news from television, radio, newspapers, and news magazines. We call these the consumer or general news media and categorize them as electronic or broadcast (television and radio) and print (newspapers and news magazines).

The print media consist of a variety of subgroups. Most widely known are the consumer publications. These include national daily newspapers such as *The Wall Street Journal, USA Today,* and *The New York Times,* as well as regional and local dailies. Another subgroup is made up of national, regional, or local weekly newspapers and news magazines.

Far more numerous than the general press are the highly specialized publications that serve the various trades and professions. These are generally called trade or professional publications. Examples are *The Journal of the American Medical Association* and *Travel Agent Magazine.*

But this is not the end of the line. In many larger cities you will find local or regional business publications. Their names frequently include the name of the city or area served, for instance, *The Memphis Business Journal.* What's more, a number of cities with a high concentration of hotels, restaurants, and nightclubs have weekly or monthly visitors' guide publications. Distributed free of charge at these outlets, they carry information on entertainment, special events, and other news of interest to people from out of town. Publications such as these frequently welcome news from hotels and restaurants.

Your target media will vary with the type of message you wish to send and the particular public or audience you need to reach. For this reason you probably will be dealing with different types of media from time to time. For example, if you come up with a new weekend package, combining an attractive room rate with theater or concert tickets, say, this should be of interest to the travel (or feature) editor of consumer newspapers, radio travel show hosts, or producers of TV or radio stations in your market area. Chances are your local newspaper, radio, or TV station usually will not be interested in such a story, because most local people seldom patronize hotels and motels in their own city or area.

Your advertising agency can supply you with the names, addresses, and telephone numbers of daily and weekly newspapers and radio and TV stations in your market area.

If you pay a commission to travel agents on all or part of the package, a slightly different version of this message or story might appeal to the editor of a trade publication written especially for travel agents. Again, your advertising agency can provide you with a list of names and addresses of travel trade publications.

Should your restaurant's chef develop a new fitness-related menu, this might be grist for the food editor's mill. Most larger newspapers and TV and radio stations have food editors, broadcasters, or restaurant critics who are always on the lookout for this kind of information.

Hotels with fewer than 500 rooms or smaller restaurants seldom have a full-time public relations person on staff or retain a public relations firm. Many do not employ the services of an advertising agency. (Some agencies have public-relations departments.)

As owner or general manager you are responsible for the image your establishment projects. You will not always be available to meet the press, therefore you might consider appointing one staff member as media liaison. Sales and marketing people are among the best candidates for this job because they are usually highly articulate and attend most important staff meetings. Accordingly, they are aware of what is going on in the property. For example, when the public relations department of Carnival Hotels & Casinos prepared its manual, it was titled "Public Relations Manual for Sales Managers," according to Beth Mignon, director of public relations. (Excerpts from the manual appear as Exhibit 11-1 in Chapter 11.) Ms. Mignon points out that "this manual was written for sales managers and/or general managers who have little or no formal training in public relations to enable them to implement basic PR principles at the property level."

It is vital to the success of your media-relations program that all employees know who the media contact person or hotel spokesperson is. What's more, they should be instructed not to talk with media representatives but to refer all press inquiries to the media contact person. Only in this way can you be assured that one voice is speaking for the establishment. The only exception to this rule would be when the spokesperson has arranged an interview for the chef, executive housekeeper, or other employee.

In developing a media-relations program, you will find it extremely beneficial to retain the part-time services of a public-relations consultant, a former newspaper, radio, or TV reporter, an editor, or a journalism student to advise your media-relations person. Should budgetary limitations make this impossible, extra care must be exercised in dealing with the media to ensure the accuracy of all information furnished to them.

In developing the press-relations campaign, your coordinator will need, at least part time, the services of a secretary or typist to prepare the basic information to be kept on file and to provide to the news media as appropriate.

To start, the job requires either a computer with a word-processing program and a letter quality printer, a word processor or a typewriter, and a photocopying machine. In addition, at the outset your media-relations coordinator should have one or two drawers of a filing cabinet.

Your media relations files should contain, at first, a supply of reprints of your latest advertising, hotel or restaurant brochures, rate cards or rate sheets, menus, any historical information on the establishment, color and black-and-white photographs, and slides of the property.

To develop a cost-effective media-relations program, the person in charge must first collect and produce basic information concerning the establishment and its staff. One of the most helpful items of media information is the fact sheet. Despite its name, this often consists of more than one piece of paper. (A sample Fact Sheet appears in Exhibit 3-1.)

Provided to a reporter or editor in advance of any interview or meeting, the fact sheet usually serves to eliminate much of the need for research on the journalist's part. It also should make any interview mercifully shorter than it otherwise might have been by answering many of the reporter's questions before the session begins.

The fact sheet should describe your property and its features to the news media. Properly written, it tells, at a glance, for example, where the establishment is located, when it was built or opened, the style of its architecture and interior decor, number and type of guest rooms or restaurant seats, number and capacities of meeting or banquet rooms, and number of employees. The fact sheet should also specify what kind of accommodations and other facilities it provides or what type of food it serves.

FACTS ABOUT THE HOTEL MAGELLAN

ADDRESS: 75 East 50th Street at Park Avenue New York, New York 10022

TELEPHONE NUMBERS: Direct dial 212-000-0000 Toll Free throughout the United States and Canada 800-000-0000

FAX NUMBERS: Reservations and Sales Fax 212-000-0000 Hotel Fax: 212-000-0000 Telex 57468

ACCOMMODATIONS: 400 air-conditioned rooms (300 units) including:
- 200 one-bedroom suites consisting of living room, bedroom, kitchenette, and bath
- 70 junior suites (large rooms with kitchenettes, sitting or dining area)
- 25 double rooms (all with refrigerators)
- 5 two-bedroom suites

FACILITIES: Color/cable TV; valet parking (garage); room service; restaurant 7 a.m. to midnight; pharmacy with coffee shop; beauty salon

SPECIAL SERVICES: International (multilingual) concierge

EXECUTIVE STAFF: Edward Jones, General Manager Irene Sharp, Front Office and Reservations Manager Helen Brown, Sales Manager

BUILDING: 26 stories; opened October 24, 1937 as an apartment (residential) hotel

- more -

FACTS ABOUT THE HOTEL MAGELLAN (continued)

ARCHITECTS:	John Cardone and Michael Mills
ARCHITECTURAL STYLE:	Romanesque
NUMBER OF EMPLOYEES:	80
MEMBERSHIPS:	American Hotel & Motel Association
	New York State Hospitality & Tourism Association
	Hotel Association of New York City
	New York Convention & Visitors Bureau
	Hospitality Sales & Marketing Association, International

Exhibit 3-1. Sample Fact Sheet.

Similar in format to the fact sheet is the outline type of staff biography. One of these should be prepared for each key executive. It ordinarily lists business experience (present and previous positions and dates of employment), education, memberships in professional organizations, and any honors or awards (see Exhibit 3-2).

Equally helpful to the news media is the narrative type of staff biography. This is written in paragraph form, usually beginning with the subject's present position, then describing his or her former jobs, education, etc. (see Exhibit 3-3).

GOOD PHOTOGRAPHY ESSENTIAL

Whether you are building a worthwhile photograph file or need to get an important photo of some special event or person, don't take chances with an amateur photographer. Editors assigned to the picture desks of major metropolitan newspa-

FACTS ABOUT EDWARD JONES

General Manager
Hotel Tip Top, Oshkosh, Indiana

EXPERIENCE:

1984–PRESENT	HOTEL TIP TOP, Oshkosh, IN General Manager Front Office Manager
1963–1984	PALOS VERDE HOTEL, Palos Verde, CA Director of Group and Agency Sales
1961–1963	HOTEL HORIZON, Chicago, IL Resident Manager
1957–1961	HOTEL SUNSHINE, Miami Beach, FL Resident Manager
1955–1957	BLACK ROCK HOTEL, Miami Beach, FL Resident Manager
1951–1955	THE ISLE HOTEL, Miami Beach, FL Resident Manager Bellman

EDUCATION:

BA Cornell University, School of Hotel Administration

MEMBERSHIPS:

Hospitality Sales & Marketing Association International,
Indiana Chapter
Hotel Executives Club
Corporate Travel Association

Exhibit 3-2. Sample Staff Biography—Outline Format.

FACTS ABOUT RAYMOND BARSTOW

Front Office Manager
Hotel Durant
Ebenezer, NH

Raymond Barstow has served Hotel Durant as Front Office Manager since December 1992.
Barstow joined the Durant as an Assistant Manager in January 1991. Earlier, he held a similar position for two years at the Lake Minnewaska Mountain House, Lake Minnewaska, NY.
He is a graduate of the Oswego College of Hotel Administration, Oswego, OH.
Barstow is a member of the Hotel Greeters of America.

Exhibit 3-3. Sample Staff Biography—Narrative Style.

pers or national news services scan hundreds of photographs daily and select only a handful of the best for publication or transmission over the news wires. Ninety-nine times out of a hundred the photos chosen have been taken by experienced professional staff or freelance photographers.

The same holds true for editors of smaller dailies, weeklies, and trade and professional publications. The only difference is that they face similar decisions with fewer photographs. This is because regardless of the size or type of the newspaper or magazine, far more photographs are submitted daily, weekly, or monthly than any editor can use.

Since competition for space is so keen, how can you be assured that your photographs will have a good chance of passing the editor's scrutiny? The best way to start is by identifying a skilled news or commercial photographer. Don't be afraid to ask for references and to check them out carefully. These are just a few of the questions you might ask of those who have done business with the candidate: Does the person have a reputation for showing up for assignments on time? Does he or she always have the right equipment available? Are the results acceptable? Are his or her rates competitive? In addition, it would be wise to inspect his or her portfolio. Make sure the photos are clear, crisp, and imaginative in composition.

Remember, when you're trying to sell a news or feature article idea to an editor, no picture is better than an amateurish one.

In planning to work with the media, make sure you have a good photograph file. This should include high-quality glossy 8×10 or 5×7 color or black-and-white prints and 35-mm color slides of interior and exterior views of the hotel or restaurant. In the case of a hotel or motel it is essential that the file include photographs of typical guest rooms, suites, meeting rooms, lobby, and dining room. Restaurants should have several views of the dining area or areas and bar and lounge taken from different angles.

Interior photography is an expensive specialty, but larger establishments find it essential to have attractive, top quality photographs in their brochures. The brochure company, your advertising agency, or interior designer can provide you with the names of qualified, experienced interior photographers. Should their fees exceed your budgetary limits, some skilled commercial photographers often can produce acceptable interior shots at much lower costs. The photographs taken for your brochure or other forms of advertising often can be used for public relations purposes.

In addition, it is useful to have on file glossy, black-and-white, head-and-shoulder portrait photos of the owner, general manager, and each department head.

Index tabs on folders in your photograph file should identify each type of view, making it simple to retrieve the desired item quickly.

If you employ the services of a public-relations professional or journalist part time, one of his or her first assignments might be to write the fact sheet and staff biography(ies) and organize the photograph file. The next step would be to write explanatory captions or cutlines for each type of photograph in your collection.

If you intend to handle these chores yourself or assign them to the media liaison person on your staff, remember to check every item carefully before giving or sending it to any editor.

If you want to become known as a reliable and accurate news source, this reputation must be earned. Remember, it is disturbing to editors to receive fact sheets, staff biographies, photograph cutlines or captions, or any other form of press information containing misspellings, incorrect names or titles, errors of punctuation, and, worst of all, misinformation.

Chances are you or your media contact person has never written cutlines for a photograph. Before starting, therefore, it is highly recommended that the caption writer read several dozen newspaper and magazine photo captions to learn how journalists capture in a few words what a photograph shows.

Then the inexperienced media liaison person should be instructed to type the caption on hotel letterhead and attach it to the back of the photograph with transparent adhesive tape. Experts say it is never a good idea to attach captions to photographs using a stapler, since a misplaced staple can easily ruin any photo.

Occasionally, a caption will become detached from the photograph. It is a good idea, therefore, carefully to *print* the name of the hotel, restaurant, or person on the back of the photograph before attaching the caption. Be sure to print the name as close to one of the edges as possible, since writing on the back of the photograph can irreparably damage it.

Do not attach captions to slides, though, because you could ruin the film. Start by printing on the cardboard edge of the slide the name of the hotel or restaurant and the room or person shown. Then put each slide into a separate envelope, together with its caption.

If you are sending a number of slides to one media outlet, you might also assign a number to each slide, print the number on the slide, and have the captions typewritten (always double-spaced). Each caption should be preceded by the number corresponding to the number on the slide it describes.

IMPORTANT: Before sending photographs to an editor, reporter, or TV news director or assignment editor, be sure to ask whether black-and-white photographs, 35-mm color slides, color transparencies, or color prints are desired.

When sending photographs by mail, messenger, or overnight delivery service, they should be protected from bending or other damage by placing two pieces of heavy corrugated cardboard in the envelope, one on either side of the slides or photographs. It may be simpler to buy photo mailer envelopes, which come with cardboard or plastic protective material.

Once you have assembled all your media information, make every effort to package it attractively. The fact sheets, staff biographies, photographs, and other materials you have prepared should be augmented with brochures, rate cards, folders, menus, and other promotional matter.

Most firms dealing with the media find it helpful to use a press kit or presentation folder to hold the media information. These folders, made of lightweight cardboard, have two inside pockets to hold the photos, fact sheets, and so forth.

A reporter or editor can easily thumb through the fact sheets and photographs in the pockets to find the information he or she is seeking. And if the writer or broadcaster is interrupted, the kit provides a handy place to file your press information until there is time to continue reading or working on it.

To identify the folder as containing news about your hotel or restaurant, try having small gummed labels made featuring your property's name and logo. These can easily be affixed to the cover of the kit. A number of these kits can be stuffed with the fact sheets, staff biographies, brochures, rate cards, weekend package flyers, and so forth. Then when a personnel appointment is made or the renovation of a meeting room or group of guest rooms has been completed, you or your media contact person should put announcements of the news into the previously filled folders and have them mailed or hand-delivered to the media. This will enable you to get the information to the news media in the shortest possible time.

Remember, as the owner or general manager of your establishment, you should review and approve all media information before it is reproduced and distributed to the press.

IMPORTANT: Before attempting to launch a media-relations campaign aimed at generating favorable publicity for your hotel or restaurant you must be certain of two things: First, that you and your media contact person are knowledgeable about the establishment. Second, that both of you are thoroughly familiar with the media you will be contacting.

To "sell" your hotel or restaurant's story to an editor or reporter, it is axiomatic that you must fully understand how the operation functions and what the building is like, be acquainted with biographical information on key employees, and have a complete grasp of the economic contribution the establishment makes to the community or area it serves. For instance, you should be able to tell media people how many jobs it created, a rough approximation of its annual payroll, and the amount of local and state taxes it pays.

In addition, the press might be interested in knowing about the ways in which the property supports local charitable organizations and the number of out-of-town visitors it serves each year. This is because visitors earn their money outside of your community, but spend it within the area. Your local or area convention and visitors bureau can be helpful in developing statistics on economic importance of your guests to the community. Its surveys usually show where their dollars are spent and how many hotel, restaurant, nightclub, retail, and other jobs they create or support.

More importantly, you must be able to tell the media people you will meet what sets your property "apart from the pack," in other words, what makes it unusual or different from other hotels or restaurants. (Advertising and public-relations professionals call this "positioning.") To accomplish this objective effectively you must be able to give media representatives important background information regarding room rates, menu prices, special package plans, meeting and recreational facilities, parking capacity, architectural style, interior decor, food and beverage outlets, and other special features of the property.

Once these first prerequisites to a media-relations campaign have been fulfilled, you should turn your attention to learning all you can about the media, with particular emphasis on your local newspaper(s) and radio and TV stations.

Start by reading the newspapers and listening to radio and TV newscasts from start to finish. After you have become thoroughly familiar with the wide variety of news and features covered in these media, try to determine where news about your establishment would best fit in. For example, if you are planning a renovation program, this might be of interest to the newspaper business editor.

But before you have a news or feature story to suggest, try to get to know the key media people and, if possible, establish a personal relationship with them. One of the best ways to start is by inviting them, one at a time, to have a brief visit or tour of the hotel or restaurant. Such a visit might include lunch, if that seems appropriate.

Don't just pick up the phone and call the editor, however. Instead, start by learning the editorial deadlines of your daily or weekly newspapers and radio and TV news broadcasts. Then make sure you call the reporter or editor well in advance of the deadline. Or, if there is no time element involved in your suggested article, you might call a couple of hours after the deadline. The reason is that as deadline hour approaches the tempo of activity in a newsroom quickens. Reporters and editors are working at a feverish pace to finish writing last-minute news stories, photo captions, or headlines before the paper "goes to press" (is printed) or the radio or TV news show goes "on the air." Thus they do not welcome calls that interrupt their concentration and, possibly, cause them to miss an important call concerning late-breaking developments in a story nearly completed. At such times you may well find them gruff and unresponsive. (For a list of the most common deadlines for the various types of media and suggestions as to when to contact their reporters, editors, and broadcasters, see Exhibit 3-4.)

In addition to the deadlines listed in Exhibit 3-4, here are a number of related suggestions.

News of a promotion geared to travel agents, for example, or anything else with a limited "shelf life," should be provided to the media four to six weeks in advance. This is because trade publication editors typically take their time in screening material to select what will appear.

For the same reason, it is recommended that when you come up with a timely article idea related to a particular holiday or other event, you should "pitch" the editor of a monthly trade publication two to four months before the occurrence.

Another source of specialized media coverage of your property's achievements or improvements are consumer or trade travel newsletters. Some are published monthly; others, quarterly. Your local librarian, travel agent, or convention and visitors bureau may be able to provide you with a list of these publications. Contact the monthlies as you would any monthly trade publication. Quarterly newsletters—like consumer magazines—work on a three-month lead time.

A phone call to the business editor of your daily newspaper, or, in the case of smaller papers, the city editor, often proves a good approach. Ask for the name of the reporter who covers news of the travel, hotel, or restaurant fields. Talk with this person and try to arrange a brief meeting in which you offer to meet his or her needs. Once you have expressed an in-

MEDIA DEADLINES

MORNING NEWSPAPERS	3 P.M. to break the following day. Reach the editor the morning before.
AFTERNOON NEWSPAPERS	9 A.M. that day. Reach the editor the day before.
SUNDAY NEWSPAPERS	Wednesday (some sections 1–2 weeks ahead).
SUNDAY MAGAZINES	4 weeks in advance.
NEWS MAGAZINES; WEEKLY NEWSPAPERS (BASED ON THURSDAY PUBLICATION DATE)	Monday. (Stories are written or rewritten Tuesday; printing and delivery take place Wednesday.)
MONTHLY TRADE MAGAZINES	Either the 1st or 15th of the month preceding cover date.
NATIONAL MONTHLY MAGAZINES (E.G., VOGUE, ATLANTIC)	Either the 1st or 15th of the month preceding cover date. However, these magazines generally work on a 3-month lead time (e.g., in April they're working on the July issue).
TELEVISION NEWS	2 P.M. that day for 6 o'clock edition. Most news conferences for TV coverage take place at 10 A.M. However, stations will work a later schedule for the 11 P.M. edition.
TELEVISION FEATURE TALK SHOWS	Book 2–5 weeks ahead of time (except for well-known celebrities). Differs for each show, so check with the producer.
RADIO NEWS	Anytime. Some are on the air 24

- more -

MEDIA DEADLINES (continued)	
	hours. All-news stations are a particularly good bet.
RADIO TALK SHOWS	Roughly 2 weeks ahead, but it varies from show to show. Again, check with producers.[2]

Exhibit 3-4. Media Deadlines.

terest in this person's work, a natural follow-up might include an invitation for a personal visit and tour of your hotel or restaurant.

WARNING: Such visits or tours are not the appropriate time to hard-sell the reporters on doing stories on your establishment. Following the tour, present your visitor with a press kit. If your invitation included lunch at your establishment, you might highlight some of your property's more attractive features after the tour. Remember, however, the real purpose of this kind of visit is to get to know one another.

To establish a lasting relationship with the news media you must learn to respect and trust each other. It is also helpful if you show an understanding and enthusiasm for each other's work.

Only through personal contact with media representatives can you find out how best to assist them in doing their jobs. It should be noted that they need article ideas as much as your property needs publicity, so your relationships with these people, properly cultivated, should be mutually rewarding. Once the media people have come to know and respect you, and realize that you will not be continually pestering them with "story ideas," you should be ready to launch your campaign.

CAUTION: Mutual respect and trust are important when dealing with media people. Make every effort to establish such a climate with your contacts in the news business. Then when you approach one of your newspaper or broadcasting friends with what you judge to be a solid news or feature story idea or photo opportunity, chances are it will be given due consideration.

But don't be deluded into thinking that your property rates an article based solely on your new relationship. The news or feature story suggestion must stand on its own merits and be measured against other available suggestions for coverage.

Remember, too, reporters and editors have their jobs to do and are ever on the lookout for ways to beat other reporters. Accordingly, never talk "off the record" with any reporter, writer, broadcaster, or editor. To put it another way, never say anything to the media that you wouldn't want to see in print or hear over the airwaves. Chapter 4 will deal with what makes news.

News articles and photos or TV and radio broadcasts offer readers and viewers facts, figures, and ideas. Favorable publicity for your establishment often results when you provide newsworthy information about the property or restaurant to the media.

As noted earlier, newspaper reporters, editors, and broadcasters are constantly working against time to meet their deadlines. So the more accurate, pertinent information you can give them in concise, easy-to-read form, the better your chances of capturing the attention of a busy newspaper or radio news editor.

With this in mind, how should you let the media know about coming events in or programs concerning your hotel or restaurant that you consider newsworthy? Many businesses supplement their personal media contacts with news releases. These are articles—written in journalistic style—submitted to the news media. They may describe improvement programs, announce personnel appointments, new rates, revised menus, or other newsworthy developments you would like customers or prospective customers to learn about.

Most experienced PR people caution against allowing people without journalistic or public-relations training to attempt to write news releases. In many cases, a poorly written or inaccurate story can do more harm than good. Fortunately, there are a number of ways in which you can get this work done. You might consider locating a retired newspaper reporter, editor, or public-relations person. A journalism student with some experience could also be helpful. Your local newspaper or your advertising agency may recommend someone interested in part-time PR work.

Except in unusual circumstances news releases are seldom issued more frequently than once every six weeks, so paying for these part-time services should not be a financial burden.

When should you favor retaining the services of a public-relations agency? Only in the case of ground breaking for construction of a new establishment, the opening of such a property, or some other important special event. Then you should contract for the firm's services for a specific period of time. It will pay you to request proposals and cost estimates from two or three agencies. In selecting bidders try to talk with businesses that have used their services to determine whether they were pleased with the results. Be sure to ask whether there were any significant cost overruns.

Your local or state hotel and motel or restaurant association may be able to recommend a public-relations agency with hospitality industry experience. This could be most helpful, since they could well have valuable media contacts that might be interested in the event you seek to publicize. See Appendix A for a list of addresses and telephone numbers of American Hotel & Motel Association Member State Associations, and Appendix D for State Restaurant Associations.

If budget limitations prevent you from getting professional help, there is another way to get your message to the news media. Instead of a news release, you or your inexperienced media contact should try preparing a media advisory or "tip sheet." This is one of the simplest and most effective ways to get a message to the media about an upcoming event at your hotel or restaurant, a personnel appointment, or the completion of a rehab program. The media advisory tells the story in outline form. It requires no more journalistic skill than to remember the reporter's six most important questions (that must be answered in every news story): Who? What? Where? When? Why? and How?

To prepare a tip sheet, write a phrase to answer each of these questions. Then have the outline typed neatly. Sending it to the media well in advance of any newsworthy event should help to generate media coverage. If it concerns the redecoration or renovation of a restaurant or lobby, the media advisory will tell when the area will be open for inspection by the media and/or the general public. Or, in the case of a person, it tells who he or she is and suggests why an interview seems warranted. It should also indicate when the person would be available for interviews and give the name and phone number of the person to contact for an appointment.

The advisory briefly describes—in outline fashion—the story and interview possibilities and/or photo opportunities. Owing to its concise format, it usually gets more attention from busy editors than a more lengthy news release. (A sample media advisory is reproduced in Exhibit 3-5.)

When you have an idea for a news story that should be of interest to a wide audience, such as an upcoming expansion program, be sure the announcement is made available to all of your media contacts simultaneously.

On the other hand, you might envision a story about a veteran employee who also happens to be a chess expert or champion golfer or has an unusual hobby, such as collecting political campaign buttons. In cases such as this it is perfectly safe to offer an exclusive article idea to one publication. Such a distinctive story likely will be of greatest interest to a feature editor or columnist, since it is not suitable for the conventional news columns.

HOTEL OR RESTAURANT LETTERHEAD OR NEWS RELEASE LETTERHEAD

CONTACT: Joe Simpson
(213) 000 0000

PHOTO OPPORTUNITY

EVENT: Nationally known sword swallower Nat Hastings demonstrates at Village Garden Club Meeting

DATE: Monday, May 14, 1995

TIME: 2 P.M.

PLACE: The Hotel Fortune Hunter, Village Room, 2nd Floor
238 Main Street East,
Alton Village

Having discussed the pros and cons of rhododendrons vs. azaleas for years, the ladies decided to offer members a little diversion at their May meeting. A tour of President Martha Jones' exquisite garden at 38-14 Semper Street will follow the meeting.

Exhibit 3-5. Sample Media Advisory.

Once you have marshalled all your facts about the person, development, or event, a phone call, personal visit, or letter might be used to get your message to the appropriate media contact.

Vital to the success of any public-relations campaign that seeks media exposure is to determine the media outlets best suited to your needs. If you are interested in attracting leisure travelers from two or three major metropolitan areas, your target media people might be the travel editors of major newspapers and Sunday magazine editors or feature editors of the same publications.

Travel sections of newspapers in your market area can be gold mines of publicity for your hotel or restaurant. But a travel editor will seldom, if ever, use a lengthy article on any one hotel or restaurant. However, there are a number of opportunities to get publicity in these widely read pages.

It will pay you, occasionally, to query the travel editors of these newspapers to see whether they are planning "destination articles" on your city or area. These usually are feature-length pieces telling prospective visitors about things to see or do in the subject locale. Many travel sections include in such articles—or in accompanying boxes or panels—information on local restaurants and hotels.

A story titled "New England's Art Secret," describing art and antique galleries in Kent, Connecticut, in *The Boston Sunday Globe,* for instance, winds up with a paragraph on local restaurants, followed by two on places to stay. Excerpts follow:

> aside from the Village Restaurant the culinary finds in town are the reasonably priced Cobble Cookery (what a great minted pea soup!) and Stosh's Ice Cream (homemade bread and the creamiest of ice creams). The Fife'n Drum Restaurant is a good bet for dinner, and the Kent Pizza Garden is good for a tall draft beer and a mean Greek pizza.
>
> The better-known places to stay in this area are east of town, overlooking Lake Waramaug. In New Preston, The Boulders Inn combines comfort and elegance at a price ($225–$265 per couple, modified American plan), and the long-established Inn on Lake Waramaug (now owned by The Baron Group) is a full-facility resort known for its special events, such as the annual July 4th Frog Jump and Festival of Flares ($138–$299 per couple MAP). The Hopkins Inn offers 11 rooms ($57–$67) but is better known for its Swiss and Austrian menu and the beauty of its dining terrace overlooking the lake. The dining rooms at the other two inns are also open to the public.
>
> Our favorite place to stay in Kent, located on a back road less than a mile from Lake Waramaug, is Constitution Oak Farm. The

200-year-old farmhouse surrounded by 160 acres has been in Debbie and Doris Devaux's family for many years. The four rooms are furnished with antiques that have always been there, and while curtains and wall-papers match, the informal old farm-house feel of the place persists ($55–$65 with breakfast). There are also several bed-and-breakfasts north of Kent Village on Route 7: Chaucer House ($75–$80), within walking distance of the galleries; Mavis' ($85 for the first night in a room, $95 for the cottage) and The Country Goose ($80).[3]

The article's final paragraph demonstrates the value of belonging to your local travel promotion organization and Chamber of Commerce. Here's what it has to say:

For a brochure describing points of interest, lodging, dining and shopping in the area, write to The Litchfield Hills Travel Council, PO Box 968U4-5, Litchfield, CT 06759; telephone (203) 567-4506. For a brochure published by the Kent Chamber of Commerce, telephone (203) 927-1463, which rings at The Villager Restaurant. If you phone the Paris-New York-Kent Gallery (203-927-3357), Kaplan himself will probably answer. He doesn't have a secretary.

In the same issue of the *Globe,* an article points up the attractions offered visitors to Italy's Cinque Terre (the Five Lands). A box in this piece headed "If you go . . ." offers addresses and telephone numbers of these area hotels.

The Sunday Travel section of *The New York Times* runs a recurrent feature entitled "What's Doing In" (followed by the name of the city or area). An article in this series described items of interest to tourists visiting Salt Lake City, Utah. Excerpts from two prominent segments of this story follow:*

WHERE TO EAT

The elegant New Yorker, 48 Market Street, (801) 363-0166, is renowned for its attentive service. The chairs are made of cherry

*Copyright © 1992 by The New York Times Company. Reprinted by permission.

wood, and the bar and floors are marble. Fresh fish is flown in daily from Monterey, Calif. The most expensive item on the menu, abalone, an iridescent shellfish, with lemon butter and béarnaise sauce, is $44.95. Shellfish stew is $19.95; the restaurant also offers meat entrees, such as rack of lamb, for $26.95. Dinner for two, including wine but not tip, runs $100 to $130. The restaurant has an extensive wine list, with an emphasis on California wines.

Diners, sitting in overstuffed chairs, get a spectacular view of Salt Lake from the 24th floor at Nino's, 136 East South Temple, (801) 359-0506, where chicken Jerusalem in cream sherry sauce with mushrooms and artichoke hearts is $16.50. Linguine con frutti di mare, a combination of shrimp, scallops, calamari and clams, is sautéed in tomato concase and white wine, is $17.95. Dinner for two and a bottle of wine, without tip, costs $50 to $60.

Vegetarian fare with dishes from Armenia, Beirut and Morocco has drawn acclaim at the Cedars of Lebanon, 152 East 200 South, (801) 364-4096.

WHERE TO STAY

The Inn at Temple Square, 71 West South Temple, (801) 531-1000, is appointed in 18th century English style, with a mezzanine library, grand piano and fireplace. The 90-room hotel is completely nonsmoking. Double rooms start at $93 on weekdays, $72 on weekends.

The Marriott Hotel, 75 South West Temple, (801) 531-0800, a half block from Temple Square, shares a building with the Crossroads Mall, with more than 100 shops. There is a fitness room and indoor pool. Double rooms start at $108 weekdays, $69 weekends.

The Doubletree Hotel, 215 West South Temple, (801) 531-7500, a 381-room hotel with a fitness center and indoor pool, is known for its sleek lobby and full concierge service. Double rooms start at $94 weekdays and $69 weekends.

The Red Lion Hotel, 255 South West Temple, (801) 328-2000, which has 502 rooms, an indoor pool and fitness center, features live jazz on Thursday and blues music on Monday. Rates for a double room are $125 on weekdays, $69 on Friday and Saturday.

Budget: This Shilo Inn, 206 South West Temple, (801) 521-9500, distinctive for the bright red lights that outline the building's exterior, has a fitness center with sauna and Jacuzzi. Double room rate starts at $59.[4]

You should also contact travel editors of these newspapers, as well as hosts of radio and television travel shows aired in your area with news of your hotel. They are particularly interested in new packages or menus you are introducing, as well as special discount offers.

If you're not getting enough food and beverage business from local residents, then community newspaper, radio, or TV restaurant reviewers or food writers and broadcasters should be contacted. PR also can boost your dollar volume of travel agency business. Getting a favorable mention of your hotel in the travel trade press is the way to begin.

Chances are the column item that follows started with a phone call from the manager to an editor or a news release sent to the editor by a public-relations person.

> Marketwatch. . . . The recent Zagat U.S. Hotel, Resort and Spa Survey had plenty of nice things to say about the Salisbury Hotel (New York City). Among other things, the survey deemed the hotel, located near Carnegie Hall, "a terrific value" with a "pleasant atmosphere." Rates at the property start at $134 single, $144 double. Call 800-223-0680 or 212-246-1300.[5]

In cities having both morning and evening newspapers, it is important not to show favoritism in the timing of your announcements of news developments. When you send a media advisory by mail, chances are the evening newspaper will have the opportunity of using it before the morning paper, since most businesses get their biggest mail deliveries in the morning. Thus you might consider sending the next advisory by facsimile transmission in the early afternoon. This would give the A.M. paper the first chance to use it, since the evening paper would be in the process of being printed by that time.

Here are a few important DO'S and DON'TS for dealing with the news media:

- ✔ *DO* earn a reputation for dealing only in facts, not hype, in your oral and written contacts with the media.
- ✔ *DON'T* ask a reporter or editor to let you review his or her article or broadcast script before publication or use.
- ✔ *DON'T* ask, after an interview or inspection visit to the property, whether or when an article will appear.
- ✔ *DO* follow up by phone to determine whether a news release or tip sheet has been received and to see whether the reporter or editor is interested in it and would like more information.
- ✔ *DO* try to provide additional information, photos, plans, etc. requested by the media ASAP.

Getting and holding the attention of an editor frequently pays off in extra coverage. The public relations director of a large New Orleans hotel, for example, phones editors when releases or tip sheets are being mailed. She does this to alert the editor to the subject matter of the material that is on the way and to suggest, politely, that he or she be on the lookout for it.

You don't have to be a PR professional to use this technique.

NOTES

1. *Webster's New Collegiate Dictionary.* G&C Merriam Company, Springfield, MA, 1981.
2. PROTECT YOUR IMAGE: Effective Media Relations for the Lodging Industry. Copyright 12/14/87 by the Educational Institute of the American Hotel & Motel Association, P.O. Box 1240, East Lansing, MI 48826. Reprinted by permission.
3. Tree, Christina. "New England's Art Secret." *Boston Sunday Globe,* May 22, 1994, p. C10.
4. *The New York Times,* Sunday, November 22, 1992, Travel Section, p. 10.
5. *Travel Agent,* April 18, 1994, p. 113.

4

What News Is and How PR Differs from Advertising

You have identified your target media and started to develop your media-relations program. The next step toward generating favorable publicity for your lodging or foodservice establishment is to learn what makes news.

News has been defined by Webster's as "**1:** a report of recent events **2a:** material reported in newspaper or news periodical or on a newscast **b:** matter that is newsworthy **3:** NEWSCAST."[1]

What makes news, then? Just pick up your morning newspaper or watch your favorite TV newscast. You'll notice that most of the headlines and major articles in the paper and the lead stories on TV concern international quarrels or wars, government debates or corruption, crime, fires, natural disasters, and so on.

The news media feed on the unusual, the controversial, and the critical rather than the routine. Specifically, there is no news value when your hotel or restaurant provides clean, comfortable rooms or appetizing meals at reasonable prices. This is what it is supposed to do.

It is newsworthy, however, when hotel rates or restaurant menu prices outpace any increases in the prices of other services as well as most goods, when customers are treated discourteously by employees, when they are subjected to long waits to register or check out, and when what apparently are firm room or restaurant reservations or convention or banquet arrangements are disregarded. Likewise, it is news when an automobile maker recalls thousands of expensive cars to correct defects that make them hazardous to operate.

This is simply to make the point that when you read a newspaper article or watch a TV newscast concerning hotel overbooking or restaurants overcharging patrons or serving tainted food, the news media does not have it "in" for the hospitality industry. The editors and reporters are simply doing their jobs by writing about or reporting the unusual.

To avoid unfavorable publicity of this sort, you should try to make sure that your reservations department is functioning properly and that waiters or waitresses and other service people deal politely with patrons.

After guarding against adverse news articles, how do you generate favorable stories in the media? In other words, what makes news that will interest reporters, editors, broadcasters, and their readers and audiences?

Let's get even more specific. Usually editors consider something newsworthy if it

—is local
—is timely
—is unique or unusual
—affects or involves people
—provokes human emotion.

One of your most important stories, of course, and the one you can use to greatest advantage, is what sets your hotel apart from all the others—what's unique or unusual about its food service, design, decor, facilities, or staff.

Chapter 3 pointed out that beneficial publicity is one means of projecting the proper image of your property to the publics you serve or desire to serve. It also notes that to build productive media relations you must start by selecting your target media.

What does all of this add up to? It means, simply, that when your property is doing something better than most, you should determine who might be interested in learning about it.

Depending on the type and location of your property, chances are it frequently can be the source of many different kinds of news stories or broadcasts. Exhibit 4-1 suggests several different subjects of news stories or newscasts that may originate in your hotel or restaurant. A few examples follow.

The Ritz-Carlton, New York, planned to conduct a day-long etiquette course for children, ages 8–12. The class included instruction on proper table and telephone manners, and writing thank-you notes. The hotel offered the story to a number of news outlets, including *The New York Times*. A *Times* editor recognized it as something that would catch the eyes of many of its well-to-do readers who are parents of preteens.

The result was that a *Times* photographer took several photos of the youngsters receiving a lesson in the placement of silverware when setting a table. One of these, accompanied by a caption prominently mentioning the name of the hotel and the nature of the course, was printed in the *Times'* Metropolitan Section on Sunday, January 23, 1994.

This means that the paper's readers in the New York metropolitan area—prime prospects for patronizing Fantino, the Ritz-Carlton, New York's restaurant—had a good chance of seeing this photo. In addition, those who read the photo caption more than likely have friends who visit the Big Apple and might be inclined to recommend the hotel to them.

New York Newsday also carried a photo and article on the etiquette course, called "Social Savvy." In addition, *New York One,* a local cable news show, sent a camera crew to the hotel.

SOURCES OF NEWS STORIES ABOUT YOUR HOTEL OR RESTAURANT

1. Personnel appointments or promotions. A new general manager, owner, chef, maitre d', etc.
2. Retirement of a veteran employee.
3. Staff reorganization.
4. Plans for renovation, refurbishing, or construction of new addition.
5. Plans for a new restaurant or meeting, banquet room.
6. Changing the name of a restaurant or changing the type of food it serves.
7. Visits by special guests—well-known political leaders, entertainers, military or civilian heroes, authors, journalists, etc. (only with advance permission).
8. Employees or guests with unique or unusual occupations or hobbies (only with advance permission).
9. Unusual awards or achievements by employee(s) or the property itself. Example: some restaurants or hotels are cited by safety organizations for having the lowest number of lost-time accidents for their size class. Improved ratings by AAA or Mobil Guide, etc.
10. Participation in community fund drives and other charitable events or activities (National Cancer Society, Red Cross, Salvation Army, etc.)
11. Conventions, exhibits or banquets, meetings of out-of-the-ordinary organizations. Example: antique or classic car owners, baseball card collectors, scientific organizations, etc.
12. Openings of new restaurants, additions or completion of renovation or improvement (upgrading) programs.
13. Addition of new facilities or services. For example, health club or no-smoking rooms and such services as faster check-in and check-out, 24-hour room service, or complimentary continental breakfast.
14. Introducing a new menu—low cholesterol, low fat, low sodium, or just seasonal changes.

SOURCES OF NEWS STORIES ABOUT YOUR HOTEL OR RESTAURANT (continued)

15. New or improved amenities including hair dryers, remote control TV, video cassette players and video cassette rentals, dataports, facsimile machines, dual phone lines, speaker phones, king-size beds, enhanced lighting, full-size desks or work stations, etc.
16. Reduced weekend rates, free rooms for children accompanying parents, new package rates, revised menu prices, etc.
17. Anniversaries.

Exhibit 4-1. Sources of News Stories About Your Hotel or Restaurant.

The result was that the etiquette course was featured on its news program.

Many hotels pay commissions to travel agents. The usual rate is 10 percent. If that's what you pay, it doesn't make news. But the Sheraton Key Largo Hotel, Key Largo, Florida, earned a place in the news columns of *Travel Weekly*, a publication for travel agents, with this unusual twist. It offered to pay travel agents a $25 bonus (besides the regular commission) on "three of its two-night packages that involve stays completed by Dec. 18."[2] The article listed the names and rates of each package and gave telephone numbers to call for reservations.

How do news articles like this get into travel trade publications? The hotel's person responsible for public relations starts by contacting the publication's office and asking for the name of the reporter or editor who covers hotel news for the area in which the hotel is located. Next, the facts of the special promotion, rate change, or personnel appointment are assembled. Then a phone call to the proper editor is placed to see if he or she is interested in the story idea. If the answer is yes, a meeting is arranged, or the information is sent to the editor. A follow-up call is appropriate in the latter case to make sure all of the information has been understood.

Let's say your chef develops a new menu or decides to offer a special holiday dish. This is food news. So you or your public-relations liaison person should contact the food editors or restaurant critics of the local newspapers and radio stations. Inviting them to a preview luncheon, breakfast, or dinner to try the new menu or specialty is one way to plant a story idea in their minds.

Newsworthy events occur daily. But only those that are communicated properly to the appropriate media will ever become favorable news articles or parts of newscasts.

Renovations and other improvements may be of interest to hotel, restaurant, and travel trade publications. The same information is frequently of use to travel editors of newspapers in your market area. These redecorating, refurnishing projects and those involving structural changes usually mean jobs for local architects, interior designers, contractors, and the tradespeople they employ. What's more, this means business for local or regional furniture, fixtures, equipment, carpet, paint, and wallpaper dealers. For this reason suggest a story on your hotel or restaurant upgrading program to the business editor of your local newspaper.

When you hire or promote department heads and other supervisory employees, this should be of interest to the business editor—or in the case of a small-town paper—the city editor. Similarly, when a veteran employee retires (or dies) you have another opportunity to secure favorable media exposure for your lodging or foodservice establishment.

Also, if you have an employee with an unusual occupation or hobby, this may be worth a call to the newspaper's feature editor. Several years ago, for instance, San Francisco's St. Francis Hotel garnered coast-to-coast publicity with a story concerning one worker whose job was operating a device that polished coins. For years management of the hotel had insisted that only shiny coins be given to guests as change.

Booking a convention of hot air balloonists or an epicurean dinner for a gourmet group also may be considered newsworthy by a columnist or feature or food writer. Occasionally such organizations may have their own public-relations people who would be delighted to work with you in publicizing the association or society—and your establishment as well.

You learn a well-known entertainer, athlete, singer, etc. will be staying at your hotel or eating in your restaurant. What do you do next? Contact his or her agent, manager, or public-relations person to see if the celebrity would be willing to be interviewed. Frequently, people like that want to "get away from it all" for a weekend or short vacation. Respecting their wishes for privacy on such an occasion may win you repeat business. And on the next visit he or she may have no objection to meeting with a media representative or even several reporters.

If you have earned the respect of the media, chances are any story or newscast resulting from an interview or even a news conference in your hotel or restaurant will mention the establishment.

Chapter 6 gives complete instructions for publicizing special events. It also offers a number of examples illustrating how some hotels have capitalized on such occasions to win valuable media exposure.

Many business executives frequently confuse advertising with public relations. Now that we have explained what makes news, let's explore how PR differs from advertising.

HOW PUBLIC RELATIONS DIFFERS FROM ADVERTISING

"PUBLIC RELATIONS is not ADVERTISING. Although this is one of the most prevalent misconceptions about the field, it often uses advertising as a tool; in fact a public-relations campaign is almost always coordinated with an advertising program. But it is not 'paid-for' space and time that you buy in newspapers, magazines, on radio or television."[3]

Advertising and public relations are alike in one respect. Neither process comes with a guarantee. No advertising agency can assure its client that the public will buy the advertised product or service. And no public relations person can honestly promise you that any particular story idea or photo opportunity will result in favorable publicity for your hotel, motel, or restaurant.

How does public relations differ from advertising? Philip Lesly points out that "Advertising is an exceptionally alluring medium because it enables the advertiser to say exactly what he wants, exactly when he wants, to exactly the audience he seeks to reach."[4]

In advertising, hotels and restaurants pay the media to carry their messages. Thus the client—the advertiser—has complete control over the content of the message to be printed or broadcast. In other words, the copy (the advertising message) the advertising agency submits to the newspaper, magazine, or radio or television station must be used word for word.

Conversely, a public relations message is one for which the media receives no money. Accordingly, a news story idea concerning a convention of rare coin collectors and dealers at the Pleasant View Hotel may hit print or go out over the air waves. Or it may not. Success or failure of this communication attempt may hinge, for example, on how unusual or timely it seems to the newspaper editor or radio or TV news director.

Several other factors may influence the go or no-go decision: the number of people attending the convention, how close to press or air-time deadline the information is submitted, the number and importance of other news developments occurring that day or week, and so on.

What's more, sometimes only a portion of the intended message the hotel or restaurant manager would like to convey to readers or listeners about this event—including the hotel or restaurant's name—is likely to be used. Space considerations in newspapers and time limitations on radio and television news programs may cause editors to delete parts of the story they judge to be of least importance. A few examples follow:

REGIONAL REPORTS/HOTEL BEAT

The former Holiday Inn Crowne Plaza in Northbrook, Illinois, is now the Northbrook Hilton (800-HILTONS). . . . The O'Hare Plaza Hotel, two miles from Chicago's main airport, has become a member of the Peabody Hotel Group (800-654-9122). . . . The Chicago Marriott Downtown (800-228-9290) has introduced what it calls "guest response" technology. A 24-hour hotline allows guests to use their television sets to report problems or make suggestions for better service.[5]

ALL LOBSTER MENU AT SANS SOUCI'S FIRST ANNIVERSARY

CLEVELAND—To celebrate Sans Souci's first anniversary, Chef Didier Tsirony prepared a menu featuring Maine's most favored crustaceans, lobster. Offered on the celebratory menu from Oct. 12 to Nov. 20 were lobster consommé with ravioli and chives ($3.95); lobster salad with purple potatoes and tarragon sauce ($9.95); lobster lasagna with vegetables and basil ($11.95); and champagne batter-coated fried lobster ($17.95).[6]

Obviously, owners or managers of these hotels and the restaurant were pleased to have been mentioned in these publications. There was much more to each story, but what appeared in print was determined by the amount of space available and the editor's decision as to the importance of each item.

In addition, the newspaper or newscasts may not use your exact words or emphasize the points intended. Thus the element of control—in terms of message content—in paid advertising is lacking in public relations.

Another marked difference between advertising and public relations concerns control of the timing of message delivery.

When buying newspaper or magazine space, the hotel or restaurant determines the exact day or month of issue in which the advertisement is to appear. Likewise, in purchasing air time, the client decides not only the day of the week and the month, but the exact time of day or night the radio or TV commercial will be broadcast.

Public relations lacks advertising's tight control over the timing of message delivery. This is because once an editor has decided to use a story it is up to him or her to determine in which issue or newscast it will run or be aired. An article that appears in an early edition of a morning newspaper, for example, may be yanked to make room for late-breaking news in a later edition. Newscasts may be revised for the same reason. And there is not a thing that the hotel or restaurant can do about it.

Not everything favors advertising when it comes to influencing public opinion, however. Public relations messages are included, where appropriate, in the news columns of newspapers, the editorial sections of magazines, and in radio and television newscasts.

"Public relations is more credible than advertising, which traces directly to the core value behind public relations. Advertising conversions ignore this credibility and impact generated by positive editorial coverage." This is the view expressed by Joel Goldstein, writing in *Potentials in Marketing* magazine.[7]

The headline in *Advertising Age* reads "PR makes impressions, sales/consumers say magazine articles rank higher than ads in influencing car sales." The article that follows points out that consumers knew much about Chrysler's big new ('93) sedans before they came on the market and before the first advertisements were in print. "The awareness had come from aggressive PR. Working months ahead of the car's public introduction, Chrysler's PR teams had exposed journalists to the LH project." What's more, the same article also notes that "Carmakers are increasingly lifting quotes out of buff books (magazines for car enthusiasts) . . . to run in their ad copy. . . .

Like the pithy quotations of movie reviewers that end up selling theater tickets, the kernel comments of car journalists might provide enough third-party recommendation to move iron at the car lot. . . . half of those people seeking advice (in the magazines) actually shop for and often buy, the recommended product."

Japanese carmakers also favor PR over advertising, in some cases. The same article, for example, reveals Nissan's view "that potential Quest and Altima buyers would be more educated and more likely to consider third-party endorsements (see below) than other buyers. That meant getting product information into print."

The *Advertising Age* piece ends by noting that Nissan's customer surveys show magazine articles topped advertising "in the customers' lists of reasons for influences that lead to buying the vehicles."[8]

The value of third-party endorsement is the chief reason hotels and restaurants highly value the favorable views of travel writers, broadcasters, and restaurant reviewers.

> Third-party endorsement refers to the tacit support given a product by a newspaper, magazine or broadcaster who mentions the product (or service) as news. Advertising often is perceived as self-serving. People know that the advertiser not only created the message, but also paid for it. Publicity, on the other hand, which appears in news columns, carries no such stigma. When a message is sanctified by third-party editors, it is more persuasive than advertising messages, where the self-serving sponsor of the message is identified.[9]

The meaning of the term third-party endorsement is further clarified by veteran publicist Richard Weiner. He writes that "In communications, the first party is the speaker or source and the second party is the listener or recipient. In public relations, an intermediary is used as a communications vehicle: the source, or first party, communicates with the audience, or second party, via an intermediary third party—a newspaper, radio stations, TV stations, magazine or other medium. Because the third party exercises journalistic standards, it provides an *endorsement* by conveying the message from the first to the second party."[10]

Recognizing this, it is easy to understand why there is so much competition among public-relations people to secure the limited amount of publication space and air time for their employers or clients.

NOTES

1. *Webster's New Collegiate Dictionary.* G & C Merriam Company, Springfield, MA, 1975.
2. "Sheraton Key Largo/Slates Agent Bonus." *Travel Weekly,* March 10, 1994, p. 14.
3. Culligan, Matthew J., and Green, Dolph. *Getting Back to the Basics of Public Relations and Publicity.* Crown Publishers, New York, 1982.
4. Lesly, Philip (Editor). *Lesly's Public Relations Handbook,* 2nd ed. Prentice-Hall, Englewood Cliffs, NJ, 1978.
5. *Frequent Flyer,* November 1993, p. 62.
6. *Nation's Restaurant News,* November 29, 1993, p. 27.
7. "Measuring Public Relations Is There ROI (Return on Investment)/ Behind PR?" *Potentials in Marketing,* June 1992.
8. *Advertising Age,* March 22, 1993.
9. Seitel, Fraser D. *The Practice of Public Relations,* 5th ed. Macmillan, New York, 1992.
10. Weiner, Richard. *Webster's New World Dictionary of Media and Communications,* 1st ed. Simon & Schuster, New York, 1990.

5

Organizing to Launch a PR Campaign

In a smaller property you, as the manager, may assume full responsibility for the public-relations function. If your hotel or restaurant is large enough to have a marketing or sales department, the director of marketing or the sales manager may be given this assignment.

But as Harry Truman once said, "The buck stops here." So, ultimate responsibility for any decisions affecting your public relations efforts and programs must rest with you. Thus, whoever takes charge of public relations for your establishment will be doing so on a part-time basis. And, chances are, anyone who assists him or her will be doing so part time as well. Besides helping to plan your public-relations campaign, the person assuming command of your PR team should also serve as liaison with the news media. Chapter 3 outlined the responsibilities of this function.

You or your designated PR person cannot be available every moment of the day. For this reason, one of the members of the support or clerical staff should be selected to assist him or her. An essential element of every public-relations organization is the secretary or clerk-typist. It is he or she who keeps the media liaison person organized.

Whenever a new media contact is made, for example, the secretary or typist should be instructed to add the reporter, editor, or broadcaster to a card index or computer disk file. Information in such a file usually includes name, address, name of media outlet, phone, fax number, and possibly a notation as to deadlines, best time to call, etc.

Whenever new photos or slides of the property are taken these too must be filed for ready access. If there are more than a few photos or slides of the hotel or restaurant, these should be filed under categories such as exterior, typical guest room or suite, lobby, restaurant, name of meeting or banquet room, etc.

If press kits, brochures, menus, rate cards, fact sheets, staff biographies, and news releases are available, these should have a place in the public relations file as well.

Chapter 3—Media Relations—explained each of the above-listed items and told how to prepare them.

Correspondence with writers, editors, reporters, and radio and television news people also should be in the public-relations files.

It would be most helpful for both the designated PR person and the secetary to learn as much as possible about public relations. Reading the books, other publications, and articles listed in the Suggested References at the end of this book and this book itself, of course, is a good way to start.

Occasionally, city or state hotel/motel or restaurant associations or local Chambers of Commerce may schedule public relations speakers or panels at their meetings or offer courses for beginners. You and/or your designated PR person should attend these sessions.

If there is a local chapter of the Public Relations Society of America in your area, check their schedule of courses, workshops, and meetings and the subjects of each. For information on the location of local or regional chapters, contact:

Public Relations Society of America
33 Irving Place
New York, NY 10003
(212) 995-2230

TRAINING IN PUBLIC RELATIONS

Whatever the field of endeavor on which you choose to embark, it's always a good idea to investigate training opportunities. Remember, as a neophyte in business—and public relations is no exception—you may or will be competing with seasoned professionals. And the media relations portion of your work, arguably as important as any other phase of PR, is more competitive than most. The reason is that newspapers and news magazines have a severely limited amount of editorial space—called the news hole—every day, week, or month. Depending on the size of your town, city, or area and the number of businesses in it, competition is especially intense to get public-relations messages into this insufficient space.

It is even more difficult when vying with others for air time on radio and television newscasts. If anything, the amount of time devoted to news broadcasts is even more tightly restricted than space in the print media.

For these reasons, it is urgent that you take advantage of every possible opportunity to learn more about the techniques and strategy of public relations. One way to start is by reading your local newspapers—or national newspapers like *USA Today, The New York Times, Washington Post, Los Angeles Times,* or *Chicago Tribune*—regularly. Listen to radio and TV newscasts carefully too. Try to determine which pieces were inspired by PR people and what made editors or news directors select the articles to be written or stories to be aired. Only by doing this consistently can you learn what the news media are seeking.

Fortunately, there is another way to gain more knowledge about PR. Most universities and many colleges and community (two-year) colleges offer day or evening courses in public relations.

LET ONE PERSON DO THE TALKING

Once the property's public relations contact person has been determined, the staff should be notified. In addition, every employee should be advised not to talk with the press, but to direct media inquiries to the media liaison person. It should be emphasized that he or she is the establishment's spokesperson and is the only one authorized to give information about the hotel or restaurant to the news media.

RESOURCES FOR ASSISTANCE

If your hotel or restaurant is part of a chain, public relations assistance may be available—on request—from the headquarters office. There may be a charge for these services.

As the manager of an independent property you may get PR help from the local chamber of commerce or convention and visitors bureau. In medium- to larger-size cities or regions such organizations generally have public-relations departments. Members of such groups should feel free to ask for advice or assistance in launching PR programs or solving public-relations problems. It certainly can't do any harm to request help.

You may contact the media in person, by phone, mail, facsimile (fax), or via news releases. But first you must select the media that will be most cost-effective. This resembles planning an advertising campaign.

Start by deciding the limits of your market area and the type of reader or listener you seek to attract. Then try to determine the newspapers and magazines they are most likely to read. Next, identify the radio or TV stations your prospects seem to favor. Your advertising agency can be most helpful in providing necessary statistical data and advice.

Once you have fixed your sights on the right targets, you should start building your media lists. These should include name(s) of appropriate reporters or editors, news directors, assignment editors, etc., name of media outlet, address, telephone, and facsimile (fax) numbers. The most important type of media list to assemble will be the one you will use to call, visit, or otherwise contact the media. This information can be stored in a computer or card index file.

If you decide you'd like to mail tip sheets, news releases, fact sheets, press kits, etc. to the media, you have two basic options.

How you go about developing, maintaining, and using your media list depends on a number of factors. These include the size of your market, your public-relations budget, and the amount of part-time clerical and typing help available.

If you can afford their services, there are a number of companies in major cities that sell mailing lists of publications of all types. Still other firms will handle your mailings for you. Simply tell them the types of publications and editors you seek to reach. They will let you review printouts of these lists and tailor them to meet your needs. These companies are listed under "Mailing Lists" in the classified section of your telephone directory.

If your budget will not permit you to use these services, you can obtain the information on your own and handle your own mailings. A phone call to the editorial department of a newspaper or the newsroom of a radio or television station, for example, will get you the names, addresses, direct dial or extension numbers, and facsimile numbers of the people you seek to reach. In the newspaper office, you should ask for the above information concerning the business editor, travel editor (feature editor on smaller newspapers), or food editor.

As a nonprofessional, you will need all the help you can get in starting your first public-relations campaign. Thus you should seriously consider setting aside a sizable chunk of time to search for allies—businesses and other organizations with objectives similar to yours. Chances are you won't have to look far.

FINDING AND COOPERATING WITH ALLIES

Napoleon often gets credit for having said this, but it was actually Voltaire who wrote: "God is always on the side of the heaviest battalions."[1] This is simply another way of saying that whatever your task, chances are it will be easier and you will have much greater prospects for success if you join forces with others having like goals. And public relations is no exception.

Once you decide to launch a public-relations campaign for your hotel or restaurant, start looking for allies.

One of the best ways to begin is by contacting your state's tourism or travel promotion office—usually located in the state capital. A list of these organizations appears in Appendix B. These people work year-round to attract leisure and business travelers to your state. It is these same tourists and business executives, sales people, etc. who are the best prospective guests or customers for your hotel or restaurant.

Thus the government travel promotion officials will be happy to give you advice and statistics and suggest how best to tie in with their advertising, public-relations, and other promotional programs. Given enough advance notice, you should be able to arrange a meeting with one of the government's public-relations people.

Most states also have business or economic development departments. These government officials should be happy to work with you in developing your public-relations programs, since they share your objective of creating new business and, therefore, jobs for your state. If you go this route, be sure to ask to be put on the tourism and economic development departments' mailing lists. This will keep you abreast of the latest developments in their various promotional campaigns.

During any meeting with the state official(s), you might volunteer to work on or cooperate with any committee that develops their promotional and public-relations drives. Chances are, by doing this you may get a head start on many of your competitors, when it comes to using public-relations or other promotional ideas put forward by the state tourism promotion and business development people.

Names and addresses of these two types of government agencies are given in Appendices B and C.

Also certain to prove helpful to you are the privately sponsored national travel industry organizations. One of them, the Travel Industry Association of America, works to generate travel to and within the United States. To achieve this objective, it develops effective promotional programs for use by its members, airlines, bus operators, car rental agencies, and so on. Two other groups develop useful statistics and coordinate research. They are the U.S. Travel Data Center and the Travel and Tourism Research Association. Members of all of these organizations represent every segment of the travel industry. The main objective of these business leagues is to encourage more people to travel. When this happens, hotels and restaurants benefit. It would be difficult for you, therefore, to find a more natural ally. For a list of names and addresses of these trade associations see Appendices A and D.

Closer to home, you may also find it profitable to seek assistance from your local or area convention and visitors bureau and Chamber of Commerce. These organizations frequently work closely with the state and regional tourism promotion organizations. And many of these entities employ public-relations professionals who can offer guidance to you in planning and implementing your public-relations campaign.

These bureaus and chambers frequently organize familiarization (fam) trips to the city or area for groups of travel writers or travel agents. In many cases they also invite individual writers or agents. The bureau or chamber starts by developing a draft itinerary that includes local tourist attractions—natural and man-made—and other points of interest. If your city or area already attracts numerous tourists, another type of ally can be helpful: the supplier.

To arrange a fam trip, the bureau or chamber starts by selecting an airline or rail line to bring the writers to their destination. Then they get member firms, such as sightseeing tour operators, bus companies, hotels, restaurants, night clubs, museums, travel attractions, and others to offer complimentary lodging, meals, admission, etc.

Here's how to participate and benefit from the resulting media or travel agency exposure: Just tell the organization's marketing and public-relations people that you're willing to provide complimentary accommodations or meals to visiting journalists or travel agents.

If you are selected as one of the fam trip hosts, be sure to arrange well in advance of the tour to have the bureau or chamber allow enough time on the itinerary for a guided tour of your property. Try to have one of your most knowledgeable managers or sales people show these guests at least one each of your various types of rooms, menus, etc.

Be sure to present each visitor with an informative press kit. Some hotels wisely mail the kits to the travel writers or agents after the tour. Experienced agents and writers appreciate this gesture, because most prefer to travel light, but manage to accumulate more than enough souvenirs and literature along the way. If the tour participants will be staying more than a night, a welcome gift of a fruit basket and some inexpensive item such as a T-shirt bearing the hotel's name and logo usually is appreciated.

The sponsoring organization's public-relations and marketing people generally screen fam trip applicants to make sure the travel writers invited have assignments to write about the city or area and actually represent or regularly contribute to reputable publications. In the case of a travel agent fam trip they try to ascertain whether the agency is a member of the

American Society of Travel Agents or a similar trade group. In addition, every effort is made to determine whether the person representing the agency actually is employed by the firm.

Thus your hotel or restaurant can benefit from valuable publicity or marketing assistance by serving as one of the sponsors of such a trip.

Remember, giving a travel agent or a travel writer a good impression of a hotel can be equally rewarding. That's because travel agents, like the media, represent one of the most important publics with which you deal. If you impress a travel agent with the cleanliness and prompt, courteous service at your property, he or she is just as apt to recommend the hotel to clients as the writer is to readers.

IMPORTANT: This kind of third-party endorsement is more effective in generating new business than the finest kind of advertising. In either case, pleasing the touring agent or writer is a win–win situation for the property.

By all means make sure your property is in top physical condition and your service people well trained before you put out the welcome mat for agents or writers. Chances are they will be seeing a number of other hotels and restaurants during their stay in your city or area, and you certainly want to outshine your competitors in every way possible. This will leave your agent or writer guests with a favorable impression of your hotel or restaurant. Keep in mind that only the most memorable of the hotels and restaurants they visit will be on their lists to be recommended to clients or readers.

Hotel and restaurant associations represent another form of ally worth enlisting. These national organizations have public-relations people on staff or employ public-relations agencies. As a dues-paying member of the American Hotel & Motel Association (AH&MA) or National Restaurant Association (NRA), you can call or write their communications and public-relations professionals for help in planning public-relations campaigns related to special events, hotel openings, introduction of new menus, and so on. Their research files have proved invaluable to many operators. In some cases use

of this material has enabled managers to adapt ideas successfully used by others. Equally as important, research has shown
others how to avoid costly errors that have plagued colleagues
in similar situations. Addresses and phone numbers of these
two national associations appear on the last pages of Appendices A and D.

AH&MA, as an example, has for the last several years published, in booklet form, entries in its annual Gold Key Public
Relations Achievement Awards competition. Many of these
entries are reprinted throughout this book. A few of the state
and city hotel and restaurant associations also employ PR professionals or agencies.

Another type of ally—the supplier—includes airlines and
other carriers, (tourist) attractions, car rental firms, food,
liquor, and wine distributors, trade associations in these and
related fields, and wholesalers. Working closely with these
firms can prove invaluable in a host of different ways.

It's easy to understand why all of these kinds of firms can
be considered allies by hotels and restaurants. When more
tourists and business travelers stay in your hotel or eat in your
restaurant, you patronize these businesses, which then get additional orders for their products from you.

Suppliers also offer hotels opportunities to develop attractively priced packages that draw additional guests or customers. Airlines and car rental firms, for instance, frequently
will work with hotels, particularly in resort areas, to put together a package that includes round-trip air fare, car rental,
and a number of nights at the participating hotel. Prices of
each segment of the package usually are deeply discounted.
Each of the three allies recognizing that deals such as these
historically draw customers who would not otherwise fly,
drive, or stay in a hotel are willing to reduce their rates
sharply. Constructing such a package generally creates new
business through advertising. But it also offers public-relations
opportunities. Most travel trade publications and many consumer newspaper travel sections often publish news reports
covering these arrangements.

Following are several articles about hotel packages carried in travel trade publications:

SAN DIEGO PROPERTY LAUNCHES PACKAGES

San Diego—The Catamaran Resort Hotel here is offering two new commissionable packages available through December.

The "Sea World Getaway" package includes two nights' accommodations, two adult admissions to Sea World, hotel parking and hotel taxes for $129.50. (Discounted children's tickets to Sea World are available.)

The Catamaran's "Cruise & Stay" package includes two nights' accommodations and a 13-hour cruise to Ensenada, Mexico, plus cruise terminal transfers, hotel parking and taxes. The package costs $169.50 on weekdays and $189 on weekends.

Package prices are per person, double occupancy. Rates are slightly higher during summer. Call 800-288-0770.[2]

GOGO LAS VEGAS

Gogo Tours is offering three- and five-night vacations at Luxor and the MGM Grand Hotel, Casino and Theme Park in Las Vegas. Included are room tax, airport transfers, a coupon book and a one-day Hertz rental car. Luxor guests also get Luxor Master Passes to attractions, and MGM guests get one-day passes to the MGM Grand Adventures theme park. Rates are $93–$270 per adult, double, and $159–$495 single, depending on length of stay, travel dates, hotel and room type. Children's rates are $28–$41, with extra nights free at either property. Optional tours include Hoover Dam Express, Hoover Dam City Deluxe, Lake Mead Cruise, Grand Canyon Bus Tour and Death Valley Bus Tour, at $12.95–$69.50 per adult, half off for children. Contact your local Gogo Tours office.[3]

BOOSTING HAWAII
PARADISE ON SALE

Value Pack. To illustrate the value of choosing Hawaii, an aggressive $3 million ad campaign was implemented last winter by the HVB and participants from the private sector, helping local hoteliers put together a "value-added package" of hotel room and car rental upgrades—and promoting them through print and television advertising.

The program not only encourages visitors to return to Hawaii, but is also designed to drive consumers to travel agents. The

"Aloha Value Pack" offers upgrades for hotel rooms and car rentals by participating hotels and rental car companies based upon a minimum 5-day stay.

Pleasant Hawaiian offers a free fourth night at its **Sheraton Princess Kaiulani** in Waikiki throughout 1994, representing a savings of up to $157 per room. A 4-night package is available at $401 per person double in tower ocean accommodations. (800) 2-HAWAII.

Like most of its competitors, **Hawaiian Pacific Resorts** offers value programs throughout 1994, including a free rental car and sixth night free special. Rates begin at $69 per room.

Aston Hotels & Resorts is working with **Budget Rent-a-Car** to offer credit of up to $50 per week on a rental car. The operator of 27 condominium resorts and hotels is offering the program, without restrictions, on any car type—from economy to luxury, family van to four-wheel-drive Jeep. "The best part is, the certificate is available to all of our guests," says Ron Adams, senior vice president of sales and marketing. Aston offers one-bedroom suites from $95 per night, with an add-on of $9 per day for a rental car. (800) 922-7866.[4]

Again, allies like airlines, cruise lines, tour operators, travel attractions, and car rental companies have public-relations departments that will produce news releases featuring such packages. It's good business for them and for you. But it doesn't hurt to ask for this kind of help.

Also, if you're having a special promotion, and want to offer guests or customers inexpensive gifts, it will pay to have airlines or car rental firms as allies. They usually will be willing to offer flight bags, baseball caps, or T-shirts bearing their logos and advertising slogans to their hotel or restaurant "business partners."

Credit card companies, too, benefit when your business improves. So, even though their cards cannot be part of any package, they often will be willing to contribute gifts your guests or patrons will enjoy having or offer public-relations assistance. Keeping in close touch with all of these allies can pay rich dividends.

Hotels having their own frequent guest programs can create tie-in promotions with their airline allies. These enable guests to "earn" frequent flyer miles for hotel stays—without losing their conventional hotel stay credits. Again, it takes negotiation with the carrier, but it's easier to work out an arrangement like this with someone you've been working with before.

As we mentioned earlier, the more guests who sleep in your hotel or eat in your restaurant, the more food, wine, liquor, glassware, chinaware, and napery your suppliers can sell you.

So, when planning seasonal or other special theme dinners, wine tastings, regional or foreign food festivals, a wine-producing region's promotional association, or other food, beer, or liquor producers' or distributors' group may be willing to donate its products or offer worthwhile discounts in return for having its brands featured in your print advertising, on menus or table tent cards, or other displays. These organizations always have public-relations departments or agencies. Tapping their resources and media contacts could give you complimentary news releases that should win valuable print or electronic media exposure for your special dinners, wine tastings, or other events.

It's certainly in the best interests of your purveyors to help you sell more of their products, so arrangements should not be difficult to make.

NOTES

1. *Bartlett's Familiar Quotations,* 11th ed. Little Brown, Boston, 1941, p. 1053.
2. *Travel Agent,* July 11, 1994, p. 36.
3. *Travelage West,* July 18, 1994, p. 75.
4. *Recommend,* April 1994, p. 16.

6

Special Events in Public Relations

Few public-relations activities generate more publicity and community interest than special events.

These range from introducing a new property, publicizing a rehabilitation or redecorating project, and dedicating an addition to the hotel or restaurant, to opening a new restaurant, meeting, or banquet room. Other special events include celebrating anniversaries, capitalizing on banquets, meetings, conventions, and trade shows held in your property, contests, special days and weeks, special awards, and open houses.

Special events usually fall into one of two categories: one-time only and on-going. Ground-breaking ceremonies for the construction of a new hotel or the opening of a new hotel or restaurant, for example, would be one-time events. An annual charity golf tournament qualifies as on-going.

The first question to ask in putting together any special event is: Why this event? It's a good idea to put your objectives for the event on paper before anything else is done. Only then can you properly identify the theme of your event and start developing a program to achieve its objectives.

Two public-relations educators have this to say about the importance of setting objectives and planning for special events: "Some of the objectives of special events in community programs are to maintain or enhance community approval, correct possible misconceptions about the sponsor's organization, present the company as a good employer, and inform the community of the volume and value of the company's local purchases. One of the first requisites in creating a special event is to allow adequate time for planning. . . . After the public relations objectives and the target audience have been defined, one is in a position to begin putting together a schedule of events, a time table."[1]

Check with contractors, all department heads, civic officials, inspection agencies, etc. to make sure ample time for planning the events, completing all necessary work, and sending invitations is being allowed. In the case of an anniversary, be sure you have the proper date. Then try to find out—possibly in your local library or newspaper office—what else was going on in your community at the same time.

Make a list of these items and provide this to the news media with any other information you may send them. This sort of background information may help attract the attention of newspaper editors and radio or TV news directors or assignment editors to the event you are planning to arrange or celebrate.

In addition, by offering information on other events that took place at the time your hotel or restaurant was opened, for example, you indicate your interest in the community. At the same time, this also helps to make your observance of the event seem far less "commercial." This should make it more acceptable as a potential news story.

The American Hotel & Motel Association (AH&MA) annually conducts a "Gold Key Public Relations Achievement Awards Program." One of the categories in this competition is special events.

Following are excerpts from synopses of winning entries in the "Special Events Individual Property" classification of the awards program featuring anniversary celebrations. All other examples of special events public-relations programs in this chapter are excerpted from synopses of AH&MA Gold Key entries. The year in which each entry was submitted and the prize category are given in each summary.*

AH&MA GOLD KEY PUBLIC RELATIONS ACHIEVEMENT AWARD
1991 Honorable Mention

PROPERTY: The Drake Hotel, Chicago, Illinois

TITLE: "Memories"

AGENCY: N/A

BUDGET: $12,565.00

SUBJECT: To bring back memories to people who had visited the hotel during its 70 years.

To promote its 70th anniversary, the hotel attempted to recover as much historic memorabilia as possible.

A press release—targeted to travel writers, feature writers, social columnists, and the travel trade—was distributed—worldwide, soliciting items individuals had saved from the Drake. Guests and patrons were asked to submit such items as:

- Old Drake postcards;
- Menus;
- Old photos;
- "Borrowed" silverware, ashtrays, china, crystal, or even furniture.

---

* All Gold Key entries are reprinted courtesy of the American Hotel and Motel Association, Stars of the Industry Program. After 1991, the program was sponsored by Visa.

THE DRAKE HOTEL, CHICAGO, ILLINOIS (continued)

Individuals submitting the finest memorabilia were awarded week-long stays at Hilton International hotels in Paris, London, Brussels, Montreal, and New York, with transportation provided by an airline, as well as weekends at the Drake.

Local media representatives acted as judges. . . , and a press reception was held at the time of the judging.

The 70th anniversary search for memorabilia was also promoted by:

- Brochures on the anniversary promotion sent to the hotel's current client list;
- Stickers announcing the anniversary affixed to all hotel correspondence;
- 70th anniversary pins given to all front line employees to wear;
- Employee newsletters, although former and current employees were not eligible to win the trips being awarded for the best memorabilia submitted.

The seven U.S. Hilton International properties, all Canadian properties, and the three European hotels involved in the promotion were asked to use the 70th anniversary stickers and pins.

Stone miniatures of the hotel and marble paperweights were distributed to select clients to promote the 70th anniversary memorabilia search.

The 70th anniversary search for memorabilia resulted in considerable local, national, and international radio, television, and newspaper coverage for the hotel, reaching an estimated audience of 40 million people.

Some of the memorabilia that was submitted included:

- Wooden coat hangers with the Drake logo,
- A menu from a wedding party held in 1922,
- Numerous photographs taken at the Drake,
- Matchbooks, post cards, napkins, guest bills,
- Assorted silverware, china, and flatware.

Many of the entries were accompanied by letters that spoke of memories of the Drake.

THE DRAKE HOTEL, CHICAGO, ILLINOIS (continued)

After being displayed in the hotel lobby, all memorabilia items were returned to those who requested
their return.
Collateral items used were:

- Press releases
- Brochures
- Paperweights
- Stone miniatures
- Trips.

The next winning entry outlines a $3 million program de-
vised to exploit the 100th anniversary of a famed resort hotel.
Few hotels could afford an expenditure of this size to promote
an anniversary. But a number of the ideas the campaign employed could be adapted by smaller properties.

**AH&MA GOLD KEY PUBLIC RELATIONS
ACHIEVEMENT AWARD
Special Events**

PROPERTY: Hotel Del Coronado

TITLE: Hotel Del Coronado Centennial

AGENCY: N/A

BUDGET: $3,000,000

SUBJECT: Celebration of hotel's centennial anniversary

The Hotel del Coronado (Coronado, California) celebrated its centennial anniversary in 1988 with a year-long
program of events. A National Historic Landmark, the
Hotel del Coronado gained international attention by
focusing on events aimed at the hotel's varied markets

HOTEL DEL CORONADO (continued)

with an emphasis on publicizing its unique history and longevity.

The celebration, which lasted an entire year, kicked off with an extraordinary fund raiser the weekend of the 100th birthday, followed by various events. The event was funded for more than $3 million, raising $1.5 million for a variety of national and regional charities.

Major components of the weekend event were:

The "kick-off" weekend, which was covered by such media as "Entertainment Tonight," *People Magazine*, "Lifestyles of the Rich & Famous," Cable News Network (CNN) and *Variety*, featured an opening-night event consisting of a variety of separate scenarios celebrating the hotel's history.

The "Some Like It Hot" room was attended by stage, screen (actor) and artist Tony Curtis, who starred in the classic movie filmed at the hotel and was accompanied by Marilyn Monroe look-a-likes; "Del's Diner" was set-up as a classic fifties diner complete with tabletops shaped like 45 rpm phonograph records; "Del Morocco" was a room recreated in the likes of the famous El Morocco of New York; a turn-of-century street scene was constructed in the hotel's Garden Patio; "Wizard of Oz" was an area attended by two of the original munchkins from the "Oz" film classic; an actor look-a-like "Thomas Edison" played host to a disco boasting an elaborate light and sound system.

The following day's events included a celebrity tennis tournament, touring the bay aboard a yacht with America's Cup Skipper Dennis Conner at the helm, and a men's "smoker" while a fashion show took place under the Garden Patio tent. Later that evening, the historic Crown Room, where Charles Lindbergh was honored following his historic flight, was decorated in rose covered arbors set on tables where a grand five-course dinner was served. The evening concluded with a Vegas-style stage show featuring headliners George Burns, Dionne Warwick, Phyllis Diller, and Debbie Reynolds with Donald O'Connor.

HOTEL DEL CORONADO (continued)

Sunday brunch presented a Navy pilot air show complete with skydivers, while guests enjoyed a brunch in the hotel's Centennial Pavilion.

Year-round events included the construction of Centennial Pavilion, which was used to host various functions celebrating the anniversary; construction of a mini-museum and The History Gallery, which offered visitors a visual history of one of the nation's largest wooden buildings; a Centennial Memorabilia Contest was coordinated garnering hundreds of donations; a photo book and video of the hotel's history were created and sold as a promotional device out of the lobby shop; "Salute to the States" featured regional recipes in the hotel's restaurants; the hotel hosted a $300,000 press party for media covering the January Super Bowl with an attendance of over 500 journalists.

The hotel entered a float in Coronado's annual Fourth of July Parade; a time capsule ceremony raised $10,000 for the San Diego Historical Society; the hotel sponsored a 10K run to benefit local charities; actors portraying famous visitors to the hotel performed daily; Centennial Post newsletters provided information about the special festivities; the San Diego Padres and the Del Mar Thoroughbred Club held special promotions honoring the hotel on the occasion of the centennial; a special "100 club" program helped to interest the staff in the Centennial and selected a winner of the San Diego Convention & Visitors Bureau Perfect Host Award for 1988 from 70,000 tourist industry employees; and the U.S. Postal Service honored the hotel with a commemorative cancellation on the day of the hotel's anniversary. (1989—Honorable Mention)

1993 AH&MA GOLD KEY PUBLIC RELATIONS ACHIEVEMENT AWARDS
Special Events—On-Going—
Individual Property
Winner   Tie

ROYAL HAWAIIAN HOTEL, HONOLULU, HAWAII

The Royal Hawaiian's (Honolulu, Hawaii) "Only at the Royal" program was introduced as a special way to mark the hotel's 65th anniversary. While extra guest amenities were an integral part of the program, "Only at the Royal" included many other facets that made it a truly special event.

Known to guests and staff alike as the "Pink Palace of the Pacific" because of its plumeria-pink Moorish-Mediterranean architecture, the Royal Hawaiian has recently undergone a $10 million renovation.

Guests are greeted with a traditional Hawaiian flower lei. When they reach their guest rooms, they find a welcome gift of fresh banana bread—made from the hotel's original 1927 recipe, and a welcome note from the general manager.

Hawaiian culture and natural beauty are highlighted daily, with entertainment and displays of arts and crafts. Historical walking tours of the hotel and grounds are offered.

As part of the anniversary celebration, the hotel scheduled a number of special events, many open to the public as well as to hotel guests. Included were many that reached back into the rich tradition of the hotel, such as a live broadcast on a local radio station of a program called "Territorial Memories," an offering of pre-statehood music. A luncheon followed the broadcast.

Also open to the public was a historic lecture on the history of Waikiki which was held at the hotel which, as the one-time summer palace of Queen Kaabumanu, played an integral part in Hawaiian history. The hotel

ROYAL HAWAIIAN HOTEL, HONOLULU, HAWAII (continued)

also hosted a "Celebration of Aloha," providing space for local artists to display collections of Hawaiian-made craft items such as quilts, coconut frond dolls, and gourd items.

The public was also invited to a number of musical events staged in the hotel's ballroom.

The Royal Hawaiian's 65th anniversary was made a truly special event which, because of the enthusiastic response, has become a yearly event at the hotel. (1993 Winner—Tie)

Painstaking research is the way to start planning any special event to assure complete success. Before setting the date for a festival, restaurant opening, or other event, make sure everything will be in readiness when the spotlight of publicity is turned on the event. Also be certain that the day chosen does not fall on any important holiday or conflict with any other event planned in or near the community you serve or will serve.

A groundbreaking or opening of a new property is vital to its initial success. Accordingly, if your budget will permit, this is the time to get professional public-relations help. In many cases this is no further away than your advertising agency or nearest classified telephone directory.

For all too many hotels, unfortunately, opening day or week is the only time they get any media attention. And that's usually because when the public-relations professionals depart, the PR campaign is over. It needn't be if you'll simply put into practice the recommendations made in this book.

Regardless of whether you go it alone or have professional help, for a groundbreaking you should invite the developer, architect, interior designer, important local civic officials, your colleagues in the hospitality industry, and the news media. You should be prepared to make brief introductory remarks, ask the architect to describe the soon-to-be-built property, and estimate its construction time. But do not fall into the trap of predicting when the hotel will open.

Your chamber of commerce and/or convention and visitors bureau usually can be most helpful in assisting you as you prepare your remarks. They can help you estimate the economic value of your property to its community, that is, how much you will be paying in real estate taxes and the number of business and pleasure travelers your property should help attract to the city or area. Judging by previous experience, they can estimate the average amount a visitor to your area spends daily on lodging, food, shopping, entertainment, taxi fares, and so on. More importantly, they can help you project these expenditures to arrive at an annual estimate. Your accountant can give you a rough calculation of your annual payroll.

Be sure to remind your listeners and the media that adding a hotel or restaurant to the local scene does not boost school taxes or increase the need for police or fire protection, but should create x number of new jobs.

Provide an opportunity for the developer and one or two of the key civic leaders to speak briefly, but ask for an outline of their remarks before preparing your own, to prevent duplication. Plan to serve light refreshments and be sure to have a tent ready in case of inclement weather.

In staging the opening ceremonies, you will want to invite some of the same people and allow them to speak again. Your remarks could cover much of the same ground as on the previous occasion, but they should be updated and much more specific. The guest list also should be similar, but could well include more people.

Well in advance of the opening, your new staff people should be given tours of the property by management team members. And they should be provided with lists of questions invited guests are most likely to ask, as well as the answers to each.

Tours of the property—in groups of no more than eight or ten—should be provided. Make sure they are conducted only by your brightest and most articulate people. Refreshments should be served following the tours. These might well be more substantial than those available at the ground breaking. Many hotels and restaurants provide a buffet or sit-down luncheon or dinner on such occasions.

In both instances you should furnish press kits to the news media attending. Kits also should be sent to other media outlets invited but not represented at the opening.

If you have had professional PR assistance in publicizing these events, you should have in the kit a background news release tracing the history of the development of the property. This or another release might describe the meeting, business or recreational facilities it offers, number of rooms or seats, if it is a restaurant, color scheme(s), and names of architect, interior designer, and contractor.

At the opening you may wish to offer guests souvenirs as mementos of the occasion. These might well range from inexpensive plastic zipper envelopes holding the press kits to more costly leather portfolios bearing the property's logo. Instead, some hotels have given away attractive desk paperweights featuring the emblem in color. Others have simply offered ballpoint pens and memo pads using the same insignia.

Imagination and creativity are the keys to success in many areas of public relations. Here are just a few examples of resourceful public-relations programs that generated extensive media coverage for hotel openings.

AH&MA GOLD KEY PUBLIC RELATIONS ACHIEVEMENT AWARD
Special Events

PROPERTY: Hyatt Regency Beaver Creek

TITLE: How to Publicize an Unopened Hotel

AGENCY: Frances Borden Public Relations

BUDGET: $200

SUBJECT: To create an interesting angle to promote an unopened hotel.

In analyzing the construction of a new property for a trait that would draw attention to the public eye, Hyatt Regency Beaver Creek (Beaver Creek, Colorado) noted the resort hotel's multiple fireplaces throughout the property.

Recognizing that guests might be calling room service and asking, "light my fire," a staff firetender position was developed. Creative imaginations quickly started a promotional but genuine search for the "hottest job in the nation in a cool spot."

The promotion served as an excellent attention-getter for a resort which would not open for six months. News releases were mailed to media across the nation with headlines that read, "HELP WANTED: Firetenders—Hot Jobs for Individuals With Burning Ambition—Anyone With a History of Burn Out Need Not Apply." Classified ads utilizing copy from the news releases ran locally and as far away as Chicago and Seattle. These also served as promotional tools at a cost much less than normal advertising space.

The news releases and classified ads proved to be a magnet for job applications from all over the country. Some responses were extremely serious while others were humorous, poetic, and even submitted on video tapes. This unusual response created yet another opportunity for a news release headlined, "Red-Hot News—Firetender Job at Hyatt Ski Resort Kindled Sizzling Ambitions Nationwide."

HYATT REGENCY BEAVER CREEK (continued)

This effective public relations idea generated coverage in *The New York Sunday Times*, *The Boston Globe*, *Corporate Travel*, *Meetings & Conventions*, *Ski Magazine*, *Travel Agent Magazine*, and several local publications, along with substantial radio publicity.
Collateral items developed/used were:

• News releases.
(1990)

The same hotel also called attention to its opening later with another notable public relations idea.

AH&MA GOLD KEY PUBLIC RELATIONS ACHIEVEMENT AWARD PROGRAM Special Events

PROPERTY: Hyatt Regency Beaver Creek

TITLE: Wanted . . . A Storyteller

AGENCY: Frances Borden Public Relations

BUDGET: N/A

SUBJECT: To attract national publicity for the opening of a new property.

To attract attention to the opening of the new deluxe resort in the Colorado Rockies, and to solicit applications for a unique staff position, a national search was announced.

Since the resort was Hyatt's "tallest" property—elevation 8,100 feet—a person to tell tales "true and tall" was sought. In its search announcement, the resort stressed that it was seeking a person to tell stories from an original, even personal perspective. Thus, a person

HYATT REGENCY BEAVER CREEK (continued)

with experience and maturity might be a prime candidate, over a person with youth and enthusiasm.

The storyteller would tell stories—original or borrowed—about the West around the resort's 16-foot campfire during the summer season. On rainy nights, the storyteller would move inside in front of a blazing fire in the lobby's ten square foot stone hearth.

A press release announcing the nationwide job search was issued, listing the qualifications for the job, and quoting the resort manager.

The release generated considerable coverage in national newspapers (*Wall Street Journal*), national syndications (Knight-Ridder, Copley, Scripps-Howard) and in local newspapers, large and small, announcing the search.

It also resulted in many radio and television stories, including a number of live and taped interviews—some as long as 30 minutes—with the manager, who explained the search, and, at the same time, secured considerable air time promoting the resort.

(1991)

Two other entries in the American Hotel & Motel Association's PR awards program explained how a downtown hotel and a resort each called attention to the opening of a new restaurant.

AH&MA GOLD KEY PUBLIC RELATIONS ACHIEVEMENT AWARD
Special Events

PROPERTY: Sheraton Boston Hotel & Towers, Boston, Massachusetts

TITLE: A Steak in the Neighborhood

AGENCY: N/A

BUDGET: N/A

SUBJECT: To promote the opening of a new restaurant located in the hotel.

The new concept restaurant—a steak house—was taking the place of an Oriental restaurant that had been in the lobby of the hotel for 25 years.

A public relations and promotions campaign was initiated to strengthen the advertising and marketing plans. The campaign sought to:

- Establish instant name and location recognition;
- Solicit restaurant reviews, articles, and photos;
- Create calendars of promotional events;
- Achieve the food and beverage revenue goals.

The hotel sought to communicate the message that the restaurant was a lively, reasonably-priced establishment that offered fun for everyone, day and night, with the excitement of visiting celebrities and sports figures, special charity events, regular weekly promotions, and live radio broadcasts.

A series of press kits and photos were sent to local and national media. Press tours of the restaurant were held, with menu samplings and interviews with the chef, manager, and other staff.

The restaurant solicited media coverage with a large number of promotions. These events were either created by the restaurant, or piggy-backed on an existing event. Some of these included:

SHERATON BOSTON HOTEL & TOWERS, BOSTON, MASSACHUSETTS (continued)

- Recruiting staff on local college campuses in a limousine;
- Sport Trivia Bowl with local celebrities that was taped for broadcast on cable television;
- Special Olympics "Jingle Bell" Run;
- Latin American Professional Network events;
- Participation in Cystic Fibrosis Chili Cook-off;
- Kiev/Boston Sister City Peace Child Party.

A restaurant mascot in a steer costume appeared at various local sporting and civic events on behalf of the establishment.

The resulting coverage by electronic and print media far exceeded that (achieved by) any similar restaurant in the city, and reached the variety of target audiences needed to promote all aspects of the restaurant—luncheon, dinner, late-night, D.J. and dancing, take-out and delivery.

The success of the public relations campaign resulted in the first-year revenue for the restaurant far exceeding the hotel's forecasted goal.

Collateral items used were:

- Press releases
- Photos
- Sample menus
- Steer costume
- Calendars.

(1990)

AH&MA GOLD KEY PUBLIC RELATIONS ACHIEVEMENT AWARD
Special Events

PROPERTY: The Pointe Resorts

TITLE: The Third Annual Celebrity Chef Hall of Fame

AGENCY: N/A

BUDGET: N/A

SUBJECT: Opening of new restaurant and support of a local non-profit organization.

The Pointe Resorts (in Phoenix, Arizona) created the Arizona Celebrity Chef Hall of Fame to accomplish two goals. First, to raise proceeds for and develop community awareness and support of a local non-profit organization; and second, to showcase a new restaurant and a sister restaurant's highly acclaimed Culinary Hall of Fame menu, featuring signature items from famous restaurants across the United States.

The Third Annual Arizona Celebrity Chef Hall of Fame . . . also served as a promotion and tool for a grand opening of a new restaurant. Each week, the new restaurant and her sister restaurant promoted three different entrees from the original recipes of celebrities representing radio, television and print media.

The promotion culminated in a fundraising awards gala featuring all celebrity entrees served buffet-style. To generate additional revenue, ticket sales were encouraged by Celebrity Chefs and restaurant staff. Invitations were also sent to participating restaurant guests (using mailing list established during promotion) in addition to an extensive press release distribution.

All Celebrity Chefs were introduced at the Awards Gala by the Mayor of Phoenix, and were presented with special mementos from the event. The Mayor also presented the "1987–1988 Celebrity Chef of the Year" award. To honor the recipient's culinary talents, his recipe for "Lobster àla Dakota" (was) featured at the Pointe's restaurant throughout the year. Others were

THE POINTE RESORTS (continued)

also honored for selling the most entrees during their week of participation.

The results of the Third Annual Celebrity Chef Hall of Fame met and exceeded original goals: A donation increase of 55 percent more than previous years was raised and donated to March of Dimes; March of Dimes experienced heightened community awareness by gaining new volunteers and inquiries from potential personnel and corporate donors; 105 inches of print publicity was received valued at $8,085 and 7:15 minutes of television publicity valued at $13,350 brought a total value of $21,425 dollar value publicity received during the promotion; "Another Pointe in Tyme" was successfully promoted city wide; dinner entrees sold at Another Point in Tyme increased an average of 275 percent during the four-week promotion with a 57 percent increase in the number of celebrity entrees sold.

Collateral items used were:

• Celebrity entree menu
• Restaurant staff button
• Waiter/Waitress information card
• Awards Gala invitation
• Awards Gala ticket
• Press releases.

(1989)

Following are three more outstanding examples of special events entered in the American Hotel & Motel Association's Annual Gold Key Public Relations Achievement Awards program:

AH&MA GOLD KEY PUBLIC RELATIONS ACHIEVEMENT AWARD
Special Events

PROPERTY: Snowbird Ski and Summer Resort, Utah

TITLE: Little Cottonwood Canyon Clean-up

AGENCY:

BUDGET: $0-1,000

SUBJECT: Removal of roadside trash from local canyon.

Once a year the local community joins the resort in organizing the annual Little Cottonwood Canyon Clean-Up. This event brings together young people from around the county who team up with city and resort employees in an effort to remove the roadside trash accumulated during the season.

To add a little spice and fun to this endeavor, the resort invites a handful of local artists to join the kids. The artists advise the kids of what garbage to save for the "Garb-Art Competition," which follows the clean-up part of the day.

The program has three goals. First, to enable the kids to join the spirit of maintaining the natural beauty of the canyon. Second, to encourage creativity through the "Garb-Art Competition." Third, to simply have a good time.

The majority of the children who participate in the program return year after year. Some of these include: Boy Scout troops, County Youth Services, local schools and handicapped children.

A sample schedule for the day:

- Breakfast at the resort.
- Divide into groups and go to the assigned area.
- Return to the resort for lunch.
- A thank-you to all participants by the local mayor and resort president.
- Garb-Art competition.
- Awards ceremony.

SNOWBIRD SKI AND SUMMER RESORT, UTAH
(continued)

Many local businesses donate discount coupons, t-shirts, etc. This enables each child to receive the same prizes and a t-shirt in addition to a certificate of award.

The budget for the clean-up project ranges from $0–1,000. The amount of the expenditure depends on the quantity of donations for food, prizes and t-shirts.

The response from the participants and artists is always positive. The overall success of the program is measured by the enhanced, eye-pleasing condition of the canyon. (1989)

AH&MA GOLD KEY PUBLIC RELATIONS ACHIEVEMENT AWARD
Special Events

PROPERTY: The Eureka Inn, Eureka, California

TITLE: The Magical Spirit of Christmas

SUBJECT: To create an ongoing community event while increasing room, food and beverage sales during a traditionally low-occupancy season.

This hotel began its holiday promotion in 1983 to increase profits in December, historically a slow month, and to provide a festive atmosphere for the community. Since the promotion began, occupancy during this time has increased from 37% to 70%, and food and beverage sales have risen 172%.

Each year the theme for the holiday celebration during the Christmas season is totally different, and the decorations, activities and special attractions encompass the entire community.

In 1983, the celebration, themed "Christmas—1922," offered guests rooms at $19.22 per person and dinners in the hotel's restaurant for $19.22 for two. The highlight of this two-week celebration was a 25-foot-tall fir tree

THE EUREKA INN, EUREKA, CALIFORNIA (continued)

adorned with thousands of white lights and 1,922 live orchids in tiny glass vials. . . .

The return of passenger train service to the area inspired the 1985 "Back on Track" holiday celebration. The 24-foot-tall hotel lobby tree was decorated with four working model trains. This "special attraction" was complemented by a month of free entertainment in the lobby. An original San Francisco cable car, adapted to a motorized chassis, was used to transport over 10,000 passengers around the city. . . .

1988's "The Magical Spirit of Christmas" began with the unveiling of a 25-foot-tall white fir decorated with prancing carousel horses, porcelain figures dressed in satin and velvet, over 5,000 white lights, miles of ribbon and mylar which rotated on a low pedestal while a specially designed sound system built into the tree played Christmas carols.

The courtyard swimming pool was covered with steel I-beams over which a 60' × 44' wooden deck was built to accommodate a 14-horse, 2-chariot child's carousel from the local museum. Also on display were several antique carved horses from antique carousels, along with fairground art and memorabilia from the 1870's–1940's.

In 1986, the hotel began a Christmas Tabloid which was produced by the local newspaper. This marketing piece, supported by vendors and suppliers to the hotel, was inserted in the local paper on Sundays prior to the tree unveiling ceremony. In 1988, the hotel itself produced the tabloid which allowed for improved quality and doubled circulation to 50,000 copies, which were inserted in newspapers throughout the region. The selling of advertising space created another profit center for the hotel.

As a result of this ongoing holiday event, the hotel has given the community a unique and hospitable gift, and turned a deficit month into a profitable one.

Collateral items used were:

- National, regional and local media lists
- News releases

THE EUREKA INN, EUREKA, CALIFORNIA (continued)

- Photography
- Brochures
- Christmas tabloid
- Advertising rate sheet for tabloid
- Invitations
- Menus.

AH&MA GOLD KEY PUBLIC RELATIONS ACHIEVEMENT AWARD
Special Events

PROPERTY: Hilton at Walt Disney World Village
Lake Buena Vista, Florida

TITLE: Hurricane Hugo Relief

BUDGET: $5,000

SUBJECT: To provide relief for victims of a hurricane disaster.

With the news of Hurricane Hugo's devastating hit on the island of Puerto Rico, employees of the Hilton at Walt Disney World Village joined with Hilton management to help the victims of this natural disaster. The primary objective was to immediately supply homeless victims with blankets, clothing and food necessary for their comfort and survival.

A large wooden crate was constructed by the hotel's Engineering Department and placed directly across from the Personnel Office, near Security.

Memos to all departments announcing the immediate call for action were distributed.

A large poster was designed by a hotel employee and placed on the wooden crate to capture the attention of each and every employee as they entered and exited the premises.

HILTON AT WALT DISNEY WORLD VILLAGE
LAKE BUENA VISTA, FLORIDA (continued)

Employees brought blankets, pillows, sheets, shoes, food, aspirin, etc., from home. The hotel's Housekeeping and Laundry Departments gathered old stock items such as bed linens and towels from the hotel's inventory.

Within 48 hours the crate was filled, sealed, and shipped to Puerto Rico.

The successful special event public-relations programs outlined in this chapter feature dozens of creative ideas. Using a little imagination you can adapt many of them to assist in producing valuable publicity and, in some cases, improved community relations for your property. Chapter 9 deals in greater detail with how best to develop beneficial community relations programs for your property.

NOTE

1. Moore, H. Frazier, and Canfield, Bertrand R. *Public Relations Principles, Cases, and Problems,* 7th ed. Richard D. Irwin, Homewood, IL, 1977, p. 238.

7

Getting Your Message Across to Guests

Few will deny that travel can be educational, enjoyable, invigorating, and rewarding. Unfortunately, however, it often involves a number of hassles: airport congestion, bad weather-induced flight delays, rail equipment breakdowns, unexpectedly heavy auto traffic, and so on. It's no wonder that a good percentage of your guests or customers arrive at your property in a bad frame of mind.

These people really need a little TLC. A smile and a friendly greeting from the bellman, desk clerk, or restaurant receptionist can do wonders for weary travelers just by letting them know that they are welcome. This is your first opportunity to communicate with the newly arrived guest or customer. And it's axiomatic that first impressions are often the most lasting ones. So make sure your people let them know somebody cares.

This message can be reinforced in hotels with a brief welcoming note from the general manager in the guest room or a cheerful "Thanks for choosing our restaurant this evening," from the waiter. Some hotels offer arriving guests fresh fruit or cookies at the front desk for the same reason.

Every organization expends considerable effort to obtain customers through marketing strategies that include advertising, sales forces, trade shows, marketing research, and public relations. Numerous books, periodicals, seminars, etc. have been written or presented explaining how to obtain customers. But relatively few of these focus on how to retain customers.

Domino's Pizza estimates that a regular customer is worth more than $5,000 over ten years, underscoring the importance of holding on to him or her.[1]

An article in the *CPA Journal* for March 1994, "When Clients Leave," says, "At the same time, the financial motivation to manage loyalty factors is clear. Boosting your client retention rate has serious implications for profitability; a 5% improvement in retention rates can boost profits 15–50%. The most profitable firms have a retention rate of 93–95%, whereas the average firm has a 78–85% retention rate. Managing the process takes planning and behavioral change for both partners and staff. Measurement, setting goals, and review is the starting point."

The article further suggests three key issues in client retention:

1. Pay keen attention to your most profitable clients
2. Stay in touch and listen actively
3. Find out why clients defect.[2]

Communicating with guests or customers should be a continuous process, as long as they are in your establishment. Thus every employee should be trained and reminded frequently to greet guests cordially, to say a pleasant "good morning," "have a nice day," and so on whenever he or she comes in contact with a customer.

A guest room tent card giving the hours of service (and room location) of restaurants, room service, or continental breakfast, if you offer it, or pointing the way to a nearby restaurant if you don't serve food can be most helpful to first-time guests.

The number of ways to show guests you care is practically unlimited. You might offer—in guest rooms or at the front desk—pamphlets from the local Chamber of Commerce or convention and visitors bureau on things to see and do in your area or community. Such a practice may be beneficial in another way. Learning of visitor attractions nearby may cause some of your guests to extend their stays with you.

Some properties have found that guests appreciate the availability of a complimentary "traveler's first-aid kit." It might contain aspirin, small strip bandages, a toothbrush and small tube of toothpaste, and pocket comb, for example. This could be offered to arriving guests at the front desk.

In larger properties, especially resorts, it may be helpful to have a welcome folder giving directions to the restaurant, pool, tennis courts, etc. A note of caution, however. Don't clutter your rooms with tent cards, folders, letters, etc. Instead, try placing most of these materials in a stationery folder on top of the dresser or desk.

It is particularly important to communicate effectively with guests during renovation. Prominently posted signs should indicate that work is being done to allow the hotel or restaurant to serve guests more efficiently or effectively. And these messages should also apologize for any temporary inconvenience the improvement programs may cause.

How extensive will your rehabilitation or new construction program be? Will there be significant inconvenience to guests? Depending on your answers to these questions you may wish to consider a brief letter to arriving guests. Presented at the front desk, this could explain the reason for and extent of the construction work and the guest benefits expected.

There are plenty of reasons why we should communicate with our guests and let them know we value their patronage. Here is a most important one:

It costs five times as much to attract a new customer as it does to retain an existing one. That is the opinion of Ronald A. Nykiel, a professor at University of Houston, Conrad N. Hilton College of Hotel and Restaurant Management and formerly a marketing executive in the lodging industry, expressed in his book "Keeping Customers in Good Times and Bad" (Berkley Publishing). To keep them coming back he suggests that management provide upgrades when possible, let customers know their business is appreciated, keep customers informed of any new services that might interest them, provide outstanding service and, where possible, go beyond what the customer expects.[3]

Another equally valid argument for keeping customers (generating repeat business) is put forward by a *Fortune* magazine article entitled "Companies That Serve You Best." The article emphasizes the importance of keeping customers or generating repeat business. "Studies by Boston Consulting Group and others show customer retention results in above-average profits and superior growth in market share."[4]

A key example in this article is the success of Home Depot, a national retail home improvement warehouse chain. Home Depot ranks first in ten-year growth in earnings per share in the Service 500, tabulated annually by *Fortune*. The article points out that Home Depot spends primarily on those elements of the business that directly benefit customers. For example, the company encourages employees to build long-term relationships with customers and pays its people as partners. *Fortune* also notes that Home Depot employees are urged to talk to shoppers daily so customer needs can be met.

Your current guest really represents a dual potential. Not only is it easier to get the guest to return than to attract a new customer, as noted earlier, but the satisfied guest can recommend the hotel to potential guests. The multiplier effect of this process can be vast.

All of the ideas suggested so far in this chapter have been in the area of one-way communication.

Only by communicating with your guests and encouraging them to respond can you really determine whether you are pleasing them.

Many hotels and restaurants have found it pays to ask guests or customers to rate the amenities, services, and facilities they offer. We have seen hundreds of different types of comment cards and guest questionnaires or evaluation forms in hotel rooms or on restaurant tables. Some are mercifully brief and to the point, while others are hopelessly long, complex, and confusing. Chances are a very small percentage of the latter are ever returned.

To persuade people to answer the questions and return these forms, numerous properties offer an incentive in the form of a cash payment or rate discount. Evidence shows that for business travelers who charge hotel bills to their employers, subtracting five dollars or other incentive amounts from the total bill for returning the guest comment card or form does not produce worthwhile results. This is because the company, not the employee, saves the incentive amount. Only if he or she is offered a cash payment is there any real incentive to complete the form and give management the information it is seeking. In the case of the leisure traveler, however, any reduction in the hotel rate will serve to convince a fair percentage of the guests to fill in and return the form.

Some forms attempt to determine how guests rate employee attitude and performance.

IMPORTANT: If you choose to use a comment card or form, there is one critical question that should be prominently placed on it. Most versions of it go something like this: If you plan to return to (name of city or area), would you stay with us?

If the majority of answers to this are negative, alert, perceptive management would take immediate action to determine the reasons behind these "no" answers and attempt to remedy the situation.

There is evidence in the hospitality industry—and many others—of a wave of interest in total quality management (TQM). TQM contains within its guidelines numerous factors that influence "guest retention."

The Malcolm Baldrige National Quality Award: A Public-Private Partnership recognizes American companies that excel in quality management and quality achievement. (The Award is administered by the National Institute of Standards and Technology, United States Department of Commerce.)

The award criteria framework encompasses the following concepts:

- Leadership
- Information and Analysis
- Strategic Quality Planning
- Human Resources Development and Management
- Management of Process Quality
- Quality and Operational Results
- Customer Focus and Satisfaction

This award program allots 30%, its evaluation points to "Customer Focus and Satisfaction." This includes

- Customer Expectations: Current and Future
- Customer Relationship Management
- Commitment to Customers
- Customer Satisfaction Determination
- Customer Satisfaction Results
- Customer Satisfaction Comparison

The segment, Customer Satisfaction Results, summarizes "trends and current levels in key measures and/or indicators of customer satisfaction, including customer retention. . . . Trends may be supported by objective information and/or data from customers demonstrating current or recent (past 3 years) satisfaction with the company's products/services."[5]

Communications with guests permit assessment of service results and offer management the opportunity to make adjustments as needed. Development of a relationship with guests is an essential key to customer retention and persuading satisfied guests to recommend the property to others.

In 1992 the Ritz-Carlton Hotel Company became the first hotel group to win the coveted Baldrige Quality Award: "the Atlanta-based company manages 25 luxury hotels that pursue the distinction of being the very best in each market. It does so on the strength of a comprehensive service quality program that is integrated into marketing and business objectives. Hallmarks of the program include participatory executive leadership, thorough information gathering, coordinated planning and execution, and a trained workforce that is empowered 'to move heaven and earth' to satisfy customers. Of these, committed employees rank as the most essential element. All are schooled in the company's 'Gold Standards,' which set out Ritz-Carlton's service credo and basics of premium service"[6] (see Exhibit 7-1).

Carnival Hotels & Casinos conducts a "Public-Relations Idea Exchange" among its properties. Here's a summary of one of the programs that focuses on guest or customer relations:

On the Monday before Thanksgiving, the Holiday Inn Dayton Mall, Dayton, Ohio, honors prospective and present customers with a VIP party. The theme of the evening is the arrival of Beaujolais Nouveau. The hotel's Holidome is set with food stations featuring elaborate dishes and open bars offering Beaujolais Nouveau. Flowers, linens, and banners match the colors of the Beaujolais Nouveau label.

Local artists and galleries display their works and a jazz trio provides background music. A Dayton radio station promotes the event. One of its DJs attends and mentions the hotel in broadcasts following the event.

Customers receive complimentary bottles of Beaujolais Nouveau as they depart. Displayed during the party are menus, rack brochures, and other promotional literature, while each manager networks with those attending.

THE RITZ-CARLTON "GOLD STANDARDS"

THE RITZ-CARLTON CREDO

The Ritz-Carlton is a place where the genuine care and comfort of our guests is our highest mission. We pledge to provide the best service and facilities for our guests who will always enjoy a warm, relaxed yet refined ambience. The Ritz-Carlton experience enlivens the senses, instills well-being, and fulfills even the unexpressed wishes and needs of our guests.

THE RITZ-CARLTON MOTTO

"We are Ladies and Gentlemen serving Ladies and Gentlemen." Practice teamwork and "lateral service" (i.e., employer-to-employee contact) to create a positive work environment.

THREE STEPS OF SERVICE

1. A warm and sincere greeting. Use the guest's name, if and when possible.
2. Anticipation and compliance with guest needs.
3. Fond farewell. Give guests a warm good-bye and use their names, if and when possible.

THE RITZ-CARLTON "BASICS"

1. The Credo will be known, owned, and energized by all employees.
2. The three steps of service shall be practiced by all employees.
3. All employees will successfully complete Training Certification to ensure they understand how to perform to The Ritz-Carlton standards in their position.
4. Each employee will understand their work area and hotel goals as established in each strategic plan.

THE RITZ-CARLTON "GOLD STANDARDS" (continued)

5. All employees will know the needs of their internal and external customers (guests and fellow employees) so that we may deliver the products and services they expect. Use guest preference pads to record specific needs.
6. Each employee will continuously identify defects ("Mr. BIV": Mistakes, Rework, Breakdowns, Inefficiencies, and Variations) throughout the hotel.
7. Any employee who receives a customer complaint "owns" the complaint.
8. Instant guest pacification will be ensured by all. React quickly to correct the problem immediately. Follow up with a telephone call within 20 minutes to verify that the problem has been resolved to the customer's satisfaction. Do everything you possibly can never to lose a guest.
9. Guest-incident action forms are used to record and communicate every incident of guest dissatisfaction. Every employee is empowered to resolve the problem and to prevent a repeat occurrence.
10. Uncompromising levels of cleanliness are the responsibility of every employee.
11. "Smile, we are on stage." Always maintain positive eye contact. Use the proper vocabulary with our guests. (Use words like: "good morning," "certainly," "I'll be happy to," and "my pleasure.")
12. Be an ambassador of your hotel in and outside of the work place. Always talk positively. No negative comments.
13. Escort guests rather than pointing out directions to another area of the hotel.
14. Be knowledgeable of hotel information (hours of operation, etc.) to answer guests' inquiries. Always recommend the hotel's retail and food and beverage outlets prior to facilities outside the hotel.
15. Use proper telephone etiquette. Answer within three rings and with a "smile." When necessary, ask the caller, "May I place you on hold." Do not screen calls. Eliminate call transfers when possible.

THE RITZ-CARLTON "GOLD STANDARDS" (continued)

16. Uniforms are to be immaculate; wear proper and safe footwear (clean and polished), and your correct name tag. Take pride and care in your personal appearance (adhering to all grooming standards).
17. Be certain of your role during emergency situations and be aware of fire and life-safety response processes.
18. Notify your supervisor immediately of hazards or injuries and of equipment or assistance that you need. Practice energy conservation and proper maintenance and repair of hotel property and equipment.
19. Protecting the assets of a Ritz-Carlton Hotel is the responsibility of every employee.

From automated building and safety systems to computerized reservation systems, Ritz-Carlton uses advanced technology to full advantage. For example, each employee is trained to note guest likes and dislikes. These data are entered in a computerized guest history profile that provides information on the preferences of 240,000 repeat Ritz-Carlton guests, resulting in more personalized service.

The aim of these and other customer-focused measures is not simply to meet the expectations of guests but to provide them with a "memorable visit." According to surveys conducted for Ritz-Carlton by an independent research firm, 92 to 97 percent of the company's guests leave with that impression. Evidence of the effectiveness of the company's efforts also includes the 121 quality-related awards received in 1991 and industry-best rankings by all three major hotel-rating organizations.[7]

Exhibit 7-1. The Ritz-Carlton "Gold Standards."

Attendance grew from 250 in 1992 to 450 in 1993. The party has achieved the reputation as one of the city's premier events. Management says this offers the hotel the opportunity to show potential and present clients "what we are capable of producing."

Numerous hotels offer similar products and services. The same is true of restaurants. For this reason product differentiation has become more difficult than ever.

These similarities and the introduction of more and more brand names have complicated the building of customer loyalty. Yet with the rise in competition such loyalty has become increasingly critical to business success. In an effort to build customer loyalty, hotels have adapted the airline concept of frequent flyer programs to meet their own needs. The hotel frequent stay plans reward guests with "points" for each night's stay or amounts spent. When a guest amasses enough "points," he or she becomes eligible for merchandise prizes, upgrades, or complimentary rooms.

What's more, some hotel organizations have negotiated tie-in arrangements with airlines. These allow guests to "earn" frequent flyer airline mile benefits in addition to their other awards.

The typical independent or smaller operation can't compete at this level. However, through communications you can develop a relationship with customers that will ensure repeat business.

Following are just a few of the steps you can take to achieve this relationship:[8]

1. Identify customers and prospects by name and address
2. Establish a relationship data base (list of guests or customers)
3. Track purchases and behavior (room type or menu dish preferences, visits, inquiries, special needs, etc.)
4. Expand information on each customer/prospect by inquiry or experience with the customer

5. Develop programs to manage the relationship (newsletters, recognition, birthday cards, notice, special promotions, etc.)
6. Let your customers know they are important to you via special holiday greetings, special discounts or other offers, and/or other forms of recognition
7. Thank your customers for their business
8. Include customers in special events (openings, anniversaries, etc.)
9. Where possible, individualize your communications.

The role of public relations in seeking to ensure a positive relationship with customers is complex as the customer reaction is the sum total of facilities, service, employee attitudes, and the personal frame of mind of the customer. However, there are numerous actions that can be taken that will please the guest enough to encourage repeat business. One must assume, of course, that basic facilities and services are adequate. As pointed out earlier, public relations cannot overcome a poorly prepared meal or a dirty room.

An in-house public relations program aimed at improving guest relations might include the following:

1. Assure guests you appreciate their business
2. Recognize repeat guests or customers
3. Listen to and act on customer suggestions and complaints
4. Invite the "repeat" guests to special events to acknowledge the importance of their business to you (these might include occasional or regularly scheduled manager's receptions and special events, such as holiday parties)
5. Keep customers informed of new or improved services
6. Tell guests of potential inconveniences such as repairs underway and stress future benefits to them
7. Answer *all* inquiries, including complaints

8. Accommodate *all* reasonable requests such as room changes and meal substitutions
9. Record all complaints and suggestions since the cumulative totals may indicate the need for changes in policies or procedures
10. Empower employees to resolve customer problems or, at a minimum, be certain the employee can obtain a prompt response from a supervisor to questions or complaints from customers
11. Read comment cards and tabulate to assess trends; respond personally if appropriate
12. "Walk the talk"! Talk to customers and employees frequently to let them know you care about their opinions and to find out "what is going on"
13. Keep both customers and employees aware of "happenings" by signs, in-room letters, and employee bulletin board notices.

We have examined a number of ways to get messages regarding your property to customers. Equally important, however, is that you respond promptly to messages you receive from guests. Only when they recognize that you consider their views important are they likely to return and spread the good word about your establishment to other potential customers.

The American Hotel & Motel Association (AH&MA) considers guest relations pivotal to the success of every property. For this reason it includes guest relations as a category in its annual "Gold Key Public Relations Achievement Awards" program.

Following are excerpts from entries in this competition.

1993 AH&MA GOLD KEY PUBLIC RELATIONS ACHIEVEMENT AWARDS
Guest Relations—Individual Property
WINNER: Omni Shoreham Hotel, Washington, D.C.

The Omni Shorehams' "I'M A.O.K." (I'm An Omni Kid) was created to make young guests feel as important as the many distinguished people who stay at the hotel. The program includes activities for children in the hotel, advice from other kids on what to visit in Washington, and the opportunity to tell management what they wanted from a visit to the hotel.

The hotel began offering special summer (July/August) weekend packages for families with kids. The low-cost package included two days/one night accommodations in a mini-suite, with children under 17 free; a late (5 pm) checkout; either a family pizza party or family breakfast; free parking; and other amenities.

The program was also designed to aid students from the hotel's "partner in education" schools learn more about the hotel industry. Selected students from these schools were chosen as special children's concierges, on hand during weekends to offer the special "I'm A.O.K." programs and advice to guest children. These students, who tried out for the positions by writing "Why I would like to be an Omni Shoreham Kid Concierge" in 20 words or less, also received pool privileges at the hotel pool for themselves and their families.

Upon checking in, children in the party were given bags which included an "I'm A.O.K." button, a "newsletter," crayons, stickers, an activity sheet, and more.

The hotel took advantage of the proximity of the National Zoo and other attractions. Fifteen area shops and restaurants cooperated with the hotel in the program by offering specials to kids who wore the "I'm A.O.K." badges, and by displaying decals that identified them as participating in the program.

SHOREHAM HOTEL, WASHINGTON, D.C. (continued)

Reaction to the program was spectacular. The hotel saw an increase of nearly 22% in rooms sold during the two months the program was run. The kids who participated in the program rated it "awesome!" The hotel used the child registrations to create a new data base for birthday and holiday greetings.

1993 AH&MA GOLD KEY PUBLIC RELATIONS ACHIEVEMENT AWARDS
Guest Relations—Chain
WINNER: Hyatt Hotels

The Hyatt Hotels' "Special Agent" program was initiated to foster understanding between the lodging and travel agent industries. It features elements of recognition and education for travel agents as well as an internal Hyatt education program.

The "Special Agent" program included an exchange of personnel, with hotel staff spending time at a travel agency learning first-hand the inner workings of an agency while agents spent time touring every area of the hotel. This exchange program has led to regular contact between hotels and travel agents to discuss mutual problems and seek solutions.

Additionally, the chain distributed a set of "golden rules" for dealing with travel agents. Buttons worn by hotel employees with the "Special Agent" logo were designed to stimulate awareness of travel agents among hotel guests.

The hotel offered special "familiarization" rates to travel agents, further boosting good will among the agents for the chain. Each month, all 106 Hyatt hotels in the U.S., Canada, and the Caribbean chose a travel agency of the month, which received a certificate and further recognition from the hotel.

HYATT HOTELS (continued)

Travel agents were offered access to an educational program about Hyatt called HySchool through their Computer Reservation System.

The Hyatt "Special Agent" program, designed to assist travel agents to better serve their clients and those of the hotel as well, was considered the best this year by AH&MA's judging panel.

1989 AH&MA GOLD KEY PUBLIC RELATIONS ACHIEVEMENT AWARDS
Guest Relations
Individual Property
WINNER: Opryland Hotel, Nashville, Tennessee

Meet and Greet Program

Opryland Hotel created its "Meet and Greet" program in early 1988 to provide a way for convention and incentive groups to welcome their delegates to Nashville. The program served more than 9,500 visitors in its first year.

When special guests arrive at the airport, a group of Opryland Hotel tour guides and ambassadors attired in antebellum clothes go to the airport to welcome them. Skycaps take their luggage, and the visitors are led to waiting hotel buses. On the way to the hotel, tour guides point out some of Nashville's important sites. Once inside the hotel, bellmen take the delegates' suitcases and ambassadors lead them to the registration desk.

Another facet of the "Meet and Greet" program is the Opryland Hotel Information Center, located at Nashville International Airport. New arrivals can stop by the center to make hotel reservations, secure information about the city, and to buy tickets for Opryland USA's attractions and transportation to and from the hotel.

1989 AH&MA GOLD KEY PUBLIC RELATIONS ACHIEVEMENT AWARDS
Guest Relations
Chain
WINNER: Stouffer Hotel Company, Solon, Ohio

Commitment to Service Excellence

Stouffer has created an Office of Guest Relations, which focuses on satisfying guests and rectifying problems when guests are not satisfied.

Guest complaints are thoroughly investigated, letters of apology are sent by the president and the general manager, and the Office of Guest Relations follows up with a brief questionnaire to the guest. Stouffer's thoughtful process has helped the company regain a large percentage of once-unhappy guests.

Other aspects of the program include a corporate newsletter highlighting outstanding service; publication of monthly graphs on hotel service that help the employees chart their progress; and quarterly team meetings to evaluate how each property is doing.

1989 AH&MA GOLD KEY PUBLIC RELATIONS ACHIEVEMENT AWARDS
Guest Relations

PROPERTY: Grand Traverse Resort, ACME, Michigan

AGENCY: N/A

TITLE: Grand Traverse Resort's Destination Excellence

BUDGET: N/A

SUBJECT: Employee identification of quality-related problems within the resort.

In an effort to help monitor, maintain and improve the quality of service, cleanliness of facilities and overall ap-

GUEST RELATIONS (continued)

pearance at this lodging property, a program was developed to address and correct problems as they relate to guest service and perception. The program was coordinated in a manner that employees are given the opportunity to assist in decision making, which involved positive employee relations.

Each guest-service-oriented department, (i.e. health facilities, bellstaff, garage, housekeeping, food and beverage, concierge, front office) comprised a committee consisting of one manager of each department, one newly hired individual in that department, and three to four additional hourly employees in the same department. The resulting committees meet once a month to discuss the quality-related issues within each of their respective areas and how the problem areas affect guest service or perception.

During the monthly "Destination Excellence" meetings, committee members discuss the possible causes of the problems and solution recommendations, which are then submitted to management. Management ultimately decides upon the solution and cause identification.

Results from the "Destination Excellence" committees have resulted in many improvements including positive reinforcement of employee opinion.

1987 AH&MA GOLD KEY PUBLIC RELATIONS ACHIEVEMENT AWARDS
Guest Relations
(Individual Property)
CO-WINNERS: The Hyatt Regency on Capitol Hill, Washington, D.C. for The Children's Suite and Anaheim Hilton and Towers, Anaheim, California for The Kids Club

Two hotels, proving that great minds often think alike, were voted co-winners for 1987. While their plans had a similar theme, each property exercises creativity and ingenuity and responded to guest needs in implementing programs which not only entertain young people on vacation, but attract family-oriented guests on a regular basis. Both hotels realized that a special hotel-within-a-hotel for children is more than a baby-sitting operation. Special rooms in the hotel were set aside and designed for children's use. Special activities of all sorts were scheduled, from films and sporting events to behind-the-scenes tours of the hotels and dining on specially prepared menus. Both properties, offering the program for the first time in 1986, reported outstanding response from families and the strong likelihood of return visits.

NOTES

1. Reichheld, F.F., and Sasser, W.E., Jr. "Zero Defections: Quality Comes to Services." *Harvard Business Review,* Sept.–Oct. 1990, p. 105.
2. Filip, Christine S., Esq., President, Success Consulting. "When Clients Leave." *CPA Journal,* March 1994, p. 72.
3. Trumfio, Ginger. "Retaining Customers." *Sales & Marketing Management,* March 1994, p. 57.
4. *Fortune,* May 31, 1993, pp. 74–88.
5. 1994 Award Criteria, Malcolm Baldrige National Quality Award, NIST, Department of Commerce, Gaithersburg, MD 20899-0001.
6. *Business America,* Nov. 2, 1992, p. 13.

7. Partlow, Charles G. "How Ritz-Carlton Applies 'TQM.'" Adapted from *Cornell HRA Quarterly,* 34, 4, p. 18. ©1993 Cornell University. Used by permission. All rights reserved.
8. Adapted from Brierly, Howard M. "The Art of Relationship Management." *Direct Marketing,* May 1994, pp. 25–26.

8

Employee Relations and Its Role in Public Relations

Chapter 1 pointed out that one of the most important "publics" hotels and restaurants deal with is their employees. Thus management should seek to communicate effectively with them as one of the early steps in any public-relations program. Keep in mind that your hospitality organization cannot achieve its goals unless rank-and-file employees deliver customer-pleasing courtesy and service. Why? Simply because it is the room clerk, restaurant server, or housekeeper who is in daily contact with your guests or patrons.

Make your staff aware that people do not travel hundreds of miles seeking to rent a room or suite. What they are after is a night's restful lodging. Likewise, others do not drive miles out of their way simply to eat a restaurant meal. What they crave is a delightfully relaxing dining experience.

The hospitality industry is unique in the way guests and patrons judge its products and services. That is, the customer's experience and his or her evaluation of it are based on the attitude and performance of the service provider as much as on the quality of the product or service itself. For example, the way a room clerk reacts to a question about the type of room reserved or the rate charged usually leaves a lasting impression with the guest. A courteous, friendly, helpful response may well determine whether this person will come back again.

The same is true of a restaurant server's reply to the customer who complains that the dish has not been prepared as ordered. A prompt, solicitous acknowledgment and a friendly attitude may help make amends for another's error.

Unfortunately, unlike most other industries, hotels and restaurants seldom have a second chance to measure up to the customer's expectations. The restaurant cook has only one real chance to prepare the dish the way the customer ordered it. Likewise, the housekeeper has only one opportunity to make the bed properly or be certain the bathroom is spotlessly clean. Of course, another steak can be grilled, a bed remade, or a bathroom recleaned. But each of these activities entails delaying the customer's or guest's satisfaction and is seldom conducive to repeat business.

When a recently purchased appliance does not work, it can be exchanged at a later date. But the overnight stay at a hotel or a visit to a restaurant provides a one-time opportunity to deliver a satisfactory or memorable product or service. Once the customer leaves the hotel or restaurant dissatisfied, there is little likelihood of a repeat sale.

To serve the customer effectively, the employee needs not only to understand the technical aspects of his or her job, but also to understand (and believe in) the mission of the organization and its concepts of service, and be able to deliver the desired high quality service expected by the customer. In addition, the employee must understand his or her options to satisfy the customers, for example, by changing a room assignment, if the guest does not like the room, or offering a complimentary appetizer if the entree order is delayed. If the employee is not so empowered, at a minimum he or she should know where to get a prompt decision. This ability to satisfy the customer may provide a competitive advantage that will result in repeat business and referrals.

To be properly motivated to provide top-notch product or service, the employees must know that management cares about them as individuals and understand the terms of employment (wages, benefits, attendance/absence rules, dress codes, complaint procedures, etc.). Also, the employee must know where to seek counseling and assistance when in-house (personal) issues affect the ability to perform the job well.

Buying a meal or a night's lodging, like going to a movie or a play, involves an intangible experience. What's more, the way in which the customer evaluates this experience is subjective at best.

How the customer reacts to the food and drink or the hotel stay may vary with a number of factors. These might include the timeliness of the service, the actions and capability of the server, the cleanliness of the property, the decor, or the attitude and circumstances of the customer.

No two people—customers or servers—are alike. Thus the differences in customers, as well as changes in their moods, attitudes, and immediate circumstances, often may determine how the performance of the waiter or housekeeper is perceived. Someone who is tired after a long, possibly delayed, airline flight might require unusually attentive service.

Most organizations have training programs aimed at teaching workers how to perform their assigned tasks correctly. But the variables mentioned above can influence how the customer or guest reacts to the service provided.

When you train employees to do their jobs better, you are improving your relations with one of your most important publics—your workers. This is because you are giving them a better opportunity to achieve job satisfaction and, possibly, prepare them for advancement.

Equally as important from a public relations point of view, you are simultaneously improving guest relations. Guests like nothing better than clean rooms and food served as ordered. This promotes the best kind of public relations and helps build repeat business.

Improving relations with employees can be instrumental in achieving a productive and effective workforce. Management should try to communicate effectively with employees to keep them abreast of

- current and future state of the business
- current and future state of the competition
- community concerns that affect the business
- changes in the property's personnel and facilities
- data on future bookings, such as conferences and social events
- staff achievements at work and outside of work
- training and advancement opportunities
- staff marriages, births, children's activities, accomplishments, and other significant happenings
- information on former employees.

Communicating this sort of information lets workers know you value them as individuals and will help develop an organizational climate that tends to motivate employees to recognize the common task of all to satisfy customers and ensure repeat visits and referrals.

There are numerous ways to get management's message to workers. These include

- discussion with supervisors (one on one)
- group meetings
- bulletin board notices
- employee handbook
- employee newsletter
- annual or periodic business status report
- bulletins/newsletters to employees' homes
- orientation and review sessions
- training meetings
- news releases to local papers, radio, and TV [circulate photocopies to employees, post on bulletin board(s)]

- interviews with news media
- talks to local business, fraternal, and social organizations (often covered by the media)
- union leaders (if organized)
- social affairs for employees (picnics, athletic programs).

Providing information of this sort to employees can provide a feeling of satisfaction on the part of both management and employees that is generally recognized as being of great value. However, it is equally important to respond to the needs of employees to communicate with their superiors. This can be done not only by training managers to be effective listeners, but to use some of the following to obtain information about employees' needs and opinions of others who know the organization and its employees:

- discussions with employees(s)
- small group meetings
- open forums
- opinion surveys
- focus groups[1]
- exit interviews
- talks with suppliers, employment agencies, union leaders (if organized), neighbors (business and personal)
- media commentary.

Task force groups with defined responsibilities can also provide broader insights into existing and potentially troublesome issues such as working conditions, availability of work-related equipment and supplies, new competition in the area, and economic downturns.

As we have demonstrated, the role of the employee is critical to the success of the hotel or restaurant. But you must communicate effectively with your people to let them know you understand this and that you recognize the solid contribution they are making—or could be making—to the success of the property. These steps will provide the employee with the knowledge, tools, and motivation to serve the customer well. This will result in an improved flow of suggestions, constructive criticism, better customer service, and, overall, a more complete understanding of the operation by each worker. A sense of belonging and "owning" among employees can be ensured by taking advantage of these public-relations techniques.

As part of its two-year-old public-relations program, New York City's independent Salisbury Hotel decided to communicate more effectively with its employees.

An old bulletin board in a low-traffic area carried required legal notices and occasional tidbits of information. A new, larger, glass-covered bulletin board was installed in a high-traffic basement location and a nearby ceiling light fixture was replaced with a bright spotlight aimed directly at the board.

Guests frequently praise an employee by name on a comment card or letter or give other reasons why they enjoyed their stay at the hotel. The card or note is then enlarged, significant portions are highlighted, and a catchy headline is printed atop it. When several messages have been similarly treated, they are prominently displayed on the bulletin board. Accompanying them is a message from management. This thanks the cited employees for their solid contributions to the hotel's continuing success and encourages others to follow their example. What's more, the hotel often receives favorable publicity in the trade or consumer news media. Reprints of these articles are given similar art treatment and posted on the bulletin board.

Salisbury management next realized that doing a better job of communicating with employees was only one part of its public-relations task concerning that public. So it launched an employee recognition program featuring length-of-service awards.

These awards consist of lapel pins bearing the hotel's logo. Workers with five to nine years of service receive plain pins. Those having completed longer tenure get pins embellished with one, two, or three semiprecious gemstones. Those with the hotel 25 years or more earn diamond-studded pins.

Awards are presented at a holiday employee luncheon. Also inaugurated at the luncheon was an employee of the year presentation. The first recipient also had the longest record of service with the hotel. She received a cash gift in addition to a plaque. Photographs were taken of each person accepting his or her award. These, too, were displayed on the bulletin board and extra copies were given to each recipient.

Other organizations have successfully enhanced or revised their recognition programs by creating ways to emphasize day-to-day recognition of employees and/or create a competitive atmosphere to become the employee of the month. Two examples were reported in *Hotel & Motel Management.*[2]

> The Hotel Bel Aire decided many years ago not to continue the conventional Employee of the Month festivities. It has instituted a PATS program, symbolic for "a pat on the back." The hotel uses small, easy-to-fill-out cards that highlight the extra effort of a line employee who has gone out of his way for either a guest or another department.
>
> The employees who have received PATS during the month attend a luncheon at which they redeem their cards for awards ranging from Tiffany gifts to trips for two to Las Vegas, Dallas or San Francisco.
>
> With the heavy employee participation, management feels that its program has been a success.
>
> Highly motivated employees have resulted from the instant recognition provided by managers and guest comment cards.
>
> A Pointe Resort in Phoenix expands on the traditional employee-of-the-month fanfare by utilizing staff meetings for presentations and having department heads vote on employees nominated by management and supervisors.
>
> According to the resident manager, this event is of such a priority that the Phoenix property would not allow even a month to go by without holding it and likely weaken a valuable incentive program. The Pointe Resort offers cash rewards, (conveniently located) parking spaces and highlighted name tags.

Additional examples of successful public-relations programs aimed at improving employee relations follow:

A Florida resort suffered from too many guest complaints
and recognized that improper employee attitudes might be a
contributing factor. A public-relations consultant worked with
management and established the following goals:

1. To achieve a four-star rating for the property
2. To help employees understand the effort management
   was making to improve the resort
3. To open lines of communication between management and employees to create a receptive mindset for
   improved performance leading to better guest relations
4. To make employees realize that management wanted
   to establish a feeling of mutual trust
5. To help employees keep in mind that the guest is the
   reason for the resort's existence.

The first step toward achieving these goals was to develop
a survey to learn how employees perceive their jobs, the resort
guest, fellow employees, and supervisors and identify problem
areas. The results were discussed in small group meetings and
plans to overcome problems developed. Employee recognition
programs also were established. Guest reactions improved and
the management noted the results were positive. The property
has 150 employees.[3]

The following examples are taken from the American
Hotel & Motel Association's Gold Key Public Relations
Achievement Award program, Employee Relations category.

These awards demonstrate the essential elements of positive and effective employee relations and relations with customers and the community. These programs include establishment of common objectives, training, communications, and
recognition. The results of these efforts are improved employee performance, better customer relations, and, of course,
more profits.

1988 AH&MA GOLD KEY PUBLIC RELATIONS ACHIEVEMENT AWARD
Employee Relations
Individual Property
WINNER: Cabot Lodge/Nashville
Nashville, Tennessee

The Cabot Lodge/Nashville's "Building a Better Team" program recognizes the necessity of training unskilled and semi-skilled workers while offering incentives to keep the skilled employees with the hotel. The training program focuses on a variety of important aspects of hotel operations, from safety and security to service and management skills. The hotel also trains disabled workers to become productive employees, including offering reading courses.

Recognition plays a key role in the hotel's employee relations program. Good work is cited in the hotel's newsletter and through monthly awards, and each year National Housekeeping Week finds the employees participating in a variety of celebrations.

The program results: low turnover, employee pride in their work, and above all, happy hotel guests.

1989 AH&MA GOLD KEY PUBLIC RELATIONS ACHIEVEMENT AWARD
Employee Relations
Individual Property
WINNER: Doubletree Hotel
Salt Lake City, Utah

CARE

Although "CARE" was developed at the corporate level, the Doubletree-Salt Lake City has earned an excellent reputation through its implementation of "CARE," and

DOUBLETREE HOTEL, SALT LAKE CITY, UTAH (continued)

has won the state award for employee relations two years in a row.

The Doubletree's CARE Committee is one of the most active in the chain. It helps the hotel sponsor annual events for its employees, such as an employee-produced talent show and an annual picnic. Employees are also regularly recognized for a job well done, with monthly and annual awards and an end-of-the-year Annual Awards Banquet. The hotel sponsors a Bounty Hunter reward for employees aiding the Sales & Catering Department; and a STAR Tokens program, in which tokens redeemable for $1 are awarded to employees "caught doing things right."

The result: The hotel has provided a work environment that attracts employees and enables them to enjoy their jobs.

AH&MA GOLD KEY PUBLIC RELATIONS ACHIEVEMENT AWARD
1991 Honorable Mention

PROPERTY: Stouffer Dublin, Dublin, Ohio

TITLE: Employee Relations Campaign

AGENCY: N/A

BUDGET: N/A

SUBJECT: To make a strong commitment to providing employees with the best possible work environment.

The hotel initiated several programs and projects designed to focus on employee recognition and quality assurance.

Eight separate facets of the employee relations program included:

STOUFFER DUBLIN, DUBLIN, OHIO (continued)

- Guest Service Wheel of Fortune
  Each time an employee receives a favorable mention on a guest service card or receives a written commendation from a manager, he or she receives a star. Once an employee earns ten stars, they are given the opportunity to spin the "Guest Service Wheel of Fortune" at a bi-monthly employee meeting. The "Wheel" consists of various prizes, including a day off with pay, complimentary dinners, cash, movie passes, etc.

- Star Wars
  The hotel staff is divided into five teams. The teams compete monthly to achieve the most improvement in their guest service index rating, which is based on efficiency, quality, cleanliness, and courtesy. Names of employees on the winning team are entered into a random drawing for a special prize, including theme park passes, entertainment books, dinners, etc.

- General Manager Luncheon and Breakfasts
  Every other month, the general manager hosts a breakfast with third shift personnel, and a luncheon for 10 to 12 other employees. The employees who attend are encouraged to voice suggestions on how guest services can be improved, as well as on improved working conditions and programs for employees.

- General Manager Interviews
  The hotel's general manager has initiated a program of interviewing every prospective employee. The goal is to ensure the selection of the best candidates for employment, and to instill a feeling of pride to all new hires. Each employee is also given an opinion survey on the work environment at the hotel not long after he or she begins employment. The general manager also conducts an exit interview with all employees who leave the hotel to learn why a person is leaving, and to identify and rectify any areas that might lead to high employee turnover.

STOUFFER DUBLIN, DUBLIN, OHIO (continued)

- Management Work Projects
  One Saturday each year, the management staff participates in a work project to improve working conditions for hotel staff. Projects have included such tasks as cleaning and painting the employees' cafeteria, painting corridors in the back of the house, cleaning room service equipment, etc. The employees appear to appreciate the management staff making an effort to make their work environment better.
- Management Involvement
  Each manager is required to get involved in, and learn to appreciate, the work done by the employees. Managers are required to spend a majority of their time during weekend shifts working in an area unfamiliar to them. In addition, the general manager works an eight-hour shift in a different line position each quarter.
- Birthdays
  Employees are remembered on their birthdays by a personalized card from the general manager, along with a complimentary dinner certificate for use in the hotel's restaurant.

Collateral items used were:

- "Starpoint" awards
- Cash Certificates for complimentary meals
- Entertainment books
- Movie passes
- Employee surveys
- Guest comment cards
- Birthday cards

Although employee relations programs in hotel chains may be designed by central headquarters executives they must be implemented at the local level. The following examples emphasize employee involvement and recognition.

1988 AH&MA GOLD KEY PUBLIC RELATIONS ACHIEVEMENT AWARD
Employee Relations
Corporate
WINNER: Days Inns of America, Inc.
Atlanta, Georgia

Believing that employees are most satisfied when they are able to make a contribution to their work environment, Days Inns created employee committees—called "People's Circles." The employees meet among themselves, address their specific concerns, and make recommendations. Issues concerning the employees are thus handled from start to finish with little management input. The circles are then dissolved once the issues are resolved.

(Proof) that the program works: Every suggestion a Peoples Circles Committee has made has been accepted. Management has seen a tremendous sense of unity resulting from the groups working together toward common goals—and achieving them.

1989 AH&MA GOLD KEY PUBLIC RELATIONS ACHIEVEMENT AWARD
Employee Relations
Chain
WINNER: Harvey Hotels
Dallas, Texas

TOTAL EMPLOYEE RELATIONS

The Harvey Hotels strongly believes that an effective employee-relations program is the best single way to ensure guest satisfaction.

HARVEY HOTELS, DALLAS, TEXAS (continued)

"New Employee Orientation" sessions introduce the concept of exceeding guest expectations. Employees then compete in an "All Star Employee" program, in which recognition comes for exceeding guest expectations. Winners receive a pin, and an All Star dinner is held annually for all company winners, past and present.

A "Friendliest Hotel Contest" has employees and hotels vying for the most favorable responses on guest comment cards. Winning individuals receive a "Friendliest Hotel" t-shirt, and the hotels receive an all-employee luncheon, prepared and served by the corporate office staff.

In the "Guest Exceeder Promotion," GEE bucks—redeemable within the company—are given to employees for special efforts that lead to guests' expectations being exceeded.

AH&MA GOLD KEY PUBLIC RELATIONS ACHIEVEMENT AWARD
1991 Honorable Mention

PROPERTY: Oceans Eleven Resorts, Inc.

TITLE: N/A

AGENCY: N/A

BUDGET: $14,387.25

SUBJECT: To develop a program of employee relations that recognizes and rewards employees for excellent job performance and provides opportunities of recreation and self-improvement.

The corporation, which owns and manages six properties in Florida, has engaged in a multi-faceted program designed to bolster and maintain employee

OCEANS ELEVEN RESORTS, INC. (continued)

morale. This has resulted in a dedicated workforce, ensuring a high level of quality in guest service and accommodations.

The program consists of:

- An Employee of the Month/Year program for each of the six properties.
  Employees of the Month receive a day off with pay or a bonus, a certificate, and their photo appears in the corporation newsletters. The Employee of the Year is named for each hotel and receives a plaque and $100 cash;
- A quarterly employee newsletter is distributed in paycheck envelopes. It features company news and articles featuring employees on the job (promotions and accomplishments) and off (hobbies, community activities). The newsletter is also mailed to tour and travel customers;
- An employee wellness program, which offers seminars and activities designed for self-improvement and recreation. Called Beachside Recreation for Employee Wellness (BREW), each hotel maintains its own program. Some sample activities are:

  —Stop smoking seminars
  —Personal finance seminars
  —Aerobic classes
  —Bowling
  —Volleyball and softball tournaments
  —A week-long health fair, where employees get health check-ups in such areas as blood pressure, glucose, cholesterol, vision, heart rate, etc., offered free to employees;

- An annual picnic for employees includes food, games, and prizes;
- The corporation sponsors teams in local community events where area companies compete in athletic competition;

OCEANS ELEVEN RESORTS, INC. (continued)

- The corporation provides United Way Referral Agents with employees who might have health, family, financial, or psychological problems. Employees seeking assistance are referred to the proper U.W. agency;
- Personalized letters are sent by the president of the corporation to employees who are named Employee of the Month/Year, celebrate a service anniversary, or receive written praise from a guest;
- The largest hotel of the chain set up a separate organization called First Mates. The group acts as a support group within the chain and also promotes use of the hotel's facilities in the community.

Through the program, employees are made aware that their extra effort is recognized and appreciated. This "team spirit" has encouraged employees to take the initiative and go beyond the call of duty in providing customer service. Improved customer service as a result of the program is evident by the letters and comments received from guests.

Collateral items used were:

- Plaques
- Certificates
- Newsletter
- Cash

NOTES

1. "The most common form of qualitative research is the focus group. A focus group is six to ten people 'typical' (a judgment obtained by screening in their selection) of the type of people expected to use the product. These people are brought together in a room where a skilled moderator leads the discussion." Lewis, Robert C., and Chambers, Richard. *Marketing Leadership in Hospitality.* Van Nostrand Reinhold, New York, 1989, p. 519.
2. *Hotel & Motel Management Show Daily,* 1990, p. 62.
3. Strenski, James B., and Luer, Charlotte. "Practical Communications Techniques That Work With Employees." *Public Relations Quarterly,* Fall 1991, pp. 34–35.

9

Communicating More Effectively with Your Community

There is a slogan among business promotion people to the effect that "All Business is Local." To put it another way, everything we do, everything we hope to accomplish must first be accepted in our own community by our own fellow citizens or it is utterly meaningless.

Thus, while the local hotel or restaurant caters to the domestic traveler as well as the visitor from abroad and all may find shelter and comfort within its doors, it is, nevertheless, the local community that must first be "sold" on the value of the hotel or restaurant and its contribution to the local community's economy.

The hotel or restaurant and the community are indivisible. You will never find a prosperous operation in a depressed community. You have never yet seen a hotel or restaurant that the community failed to accept prosper, and you never will.

The hotel or restaurant has been called the hub of the community because most hotels and restaurants offer facilities for group meetings, conventions, sales meetings, banquets,

and other social functions. Many important meetings that affect the future of the city, town, or region often are held in
these facilities. These include conferences of public officials,
union–management labor contract negotiations, conventions
of local, state, regional, and national trade associations and
professional societies, as well as the regular meetings of important civic organizations and service clubs constantly striving to improve the communities they represent and serve.

Thus it's easy to see why no hotel or restaurant can succeed unless it is accepted by the community.

An experienced public-relations executive tells how this
questioning acceptance can be won: "Good community relations are not built on 'do-goodisms.' They are achieved not
simply by helping support good causes, but by assuming a role
of leadership in community affairs—by helping create solutions to community problems, by constructive planning, and
by securing the support of other citizens for worthy causes. In
brief, good community relations result from the organization's
becoming, in every sense, a good citizen."[1]

A community relations program has been defined as "a
bridge between the company and the community. . . .
Community relations, as a public relations function, is an institution's planned, active and continuing participation with and
within a community to maintain and enhance its environment
to the benefit of both the institution and the community."[2]

COMMUNITY RELATIONS CRITERIA
FOR ACTIVITIES

Lesly's Public Relations Handbook suggests the following criteria for public-relations activities: "Some of the forms action
(problem-solving and simply community-enhancing) can take
include:

1. Creating something needed that didn't exist before
2. Eliminating something that causes a problem

3. Developing means of self-determination
4. Broadening use of something that exists to include "have nots"
5. Sharing equipment, facilities, professional expertise
6. Tutoring, counseling, training
7. Reconstituting, repairing, dressing up
8. Promotion of a community outside of its confines
9. Activating others."[3]

COMMUNICATIONS

"In community relations, publicity and promotion are tools in support of an action program, not substitutes for it. A simple test for written communication used in programs is: Is the program being described one that the reader/viewer can react favorably to without additional prompting? In short, does the program stand on its own feet?"[4]

Most businesses provide some jobs for and pay taxes to communities in which they are located. But you should stress to your neighbors and other community residents that hotels and restaurants are labor intensive. This is because, despite technological advances in the twentieth century, beds still must be made, floors mopped, luggage carried, bathrooms cleaned, and restaurant tables set, served, and cleared by hand. Thus, per dollar of income, they provide employment for more community residents than most other types of businesses.

Never let your neighbors forget that hotels and restaurants attract business and pleasure travelers to your community from all over the United States and other countries as well. What's more, you should remind local people that most hotel income is earned from visitors outside the community but is spent within it.

In devising your community relations program start by listing the items your establishment provides its community/ environment besides lodging, food-service, and meeting and banquet space. These might include employment for local residents, taxes paid to the community, and attractive, well-maintained building(s).

Then jot down the things your business receives from its community/environment—employees, land, police and fire protection, water, etc.

Next, list the items your business requires from its community/environment—more employees, lower taxes, better reputation, etc.

Finally, write down management's or owner's complaints about the community/environment in which it operates: air pollution, undependable garbage pickup, lack of adequate parking space to attract more shoppers and other visitors, etc. Then try to figure out how your hotel or restaurant can take a leadership position in striving to right some of these wrongs.

Before announcing any plan, be sure to consult with officials of your Chamber of Commerce or convention and visitors bureau. Chances are you can tie in with one or more of their community betterment programs. You may also be able to convince them to support campaigns aimed at achieving one or more of your objectives.

One might ask how this affects the "bottom line." Most of the hotel's customers are from out of town, but potential visitors seek advice on where to stay from people or organizations in the community. Restaurants, of course, have a varied mix of in-town or out-of-town clientele, depending largely on location and extent of reputation. In either case, positive perceptions of the establishment should be an essential goal of every restaurant or hotel. This informed and positive opinion will result in more referrals and increased revenue.

Also, a hard-earned reputation as a good corporate citizen of the community also encourages people to apply for jobs and probably encourages suppliers to seek out opportunities to do business with the organization. In addition, whenever there is an emergency or a problem at the hotel or restaurant, having a positive public-relations standing in the community will enable the property to be evaluated fairly. If a property is unknown or is not well considered in the community, there could be an initial assumption of wrongdoing. This would make it considerably more difficult to present your side of the story effectively.

Efforts to be a good neighbor, sharing in solving community needs, making contributions in cash or in kind to worthwhile activities and programs, and urging and recognizing employee community involvement should occur primarily as a part of the ethical mission of the organization. The ability, if needed, to use the good will developed in times of public relations concerns is really a by-product of doing the right thing in the first place.

In other words, positive community relations and positive public relations are truly a two-way street.

There are many avenues leading to community involvement. Your selection might be based on current needs of the community, personal interests of the owners, managers, and employees, and resources needed and available. To meet one-time or short-term needs, you might assist a neighborhood or several families with housing or food after a severe fire. On a longer-term basis you might support reading improvement programs in local schools through contributions or staff support.

The opportunities are limitless. You and some of your staff might work with the local clergy, educators, recreation personnel, welfare organizations, athletic groups, United Fund, rehabilitation organizations, meals-on-wheels, arts activity alliances, public radio or TV, hospitals, child welfare support groups, family mediation services, and community government organizations.

Areas in which involvement currently is badly needed in many communities include education, jobs, ecology, and family support. Local Chambers of Commerce often can suggest ways to become involved.

Here's how one hotel got involved in a community-wide program and how it helped seriously ill children and itself.

Carnival Hotels & Casinos distributes public relations "Idea Exchange" forms to its properties quarterly. A summary of a report submitted by The Condado Beach Trio, Condado, Puerto Rico, follows:

The hotel participated in a "Day of Caring" sponsored by the United Way. Cooperating companies were to choose a charity and make a significant contribution to it. "Proyecto Amor," a home for children with AIDS, was selected by the Trio. Donations collected from employees and business associates—who received letters from the hotel—amounted to $15,000, enough to buy the children the playground of their dreams.

El Nuevo Dia, a major daily newspaper, devoted a three-page centerfold article—featuring color photographs—to the program. The Condado Beach Trio's role in the "Day of Caring" also resulted in articles in the *San Juan Star, El Diario,* and local magazines including *VEA* and *TV Guia.*

Following the success of the program, The Condado Beach Trio has continued its relationship with the children and has planned other activities to benefit them.

Chapter 3, Media Relations, and Chapter 4, What News Is and How Public Relations Differs from Advertising, made it clear that building a successful community relations program requires knowing the media and its needs and informing the community repeatedly about the company's mission, its contributions to the area, and its dedication to the success of the community. A deep and abiding involvement in the community will simplify getting your story to its residents and will also permit you more easily to assess the impact of your work and the changing needs of the community.

The following examples illustrate a variety of programs conducted in individual properties that successfully gained positive public-relations recognition in their communities.

McGuffey's, a chain of mostly casual restaurants headquartered in North Carolina, has as part of its mission statement "to lead the service industry to new levels of excellence through innovation and employee empowerment." The founder and CEO, Keith Dunn, says "We want to be leading citizens of each community, give something back to the communities, and spur a rise in social consciousness and commitment among our employees and customers."[5] The following programs were designed to achieve this goal:

1. In the Asheville, NC property, one four-person table is marked with a small sign noting that 10% of the check will be donated to AIDS causes. Customers may select this table and therefore contribute to this cause.
2. In a city where three of his restaurants are located, Dunn leads a coalition to build 1,000 units of moderate-income housing.
3. Dunn contributes 1% of sales to Area Betterment in the headquarters city and assists with the local cooperative day-care center.
4. Other successful community projects in which McGuffey's has participated include supporting muscular dystrophy research, sponsoring street festivals, and contributing proceeds to charities and activities like a Junior Achievement chapter.
5. On Thanksgiving McGuffey's closes its restaurants to serve Thanksgiving dinner to the homeless and needy.

These activities send a message to the community that McGuffey's is a good corporate citizen and the restaurants may well benefit by increased business and excellent relationships with suppliers and potential employees.

The Ritz-Carlton Philadelphia recently announced that it has translated its room service menu and guest services directory into Braille. Officials decided to offer this new service as part of its commitment to the Americans with Disabilities Act, according to a hotel spokesperson. The Jenny Beck Braille Center in Philadelphia assisted the hotel in the change.[6]

Doral Hotels & Resorts, based in Manhattan, recently announced a program that will provide up to 180 room-nights a year to cancer patients and their families. The Doral Hospitality Program will be jointly administered by Doral's New York properties and the Kaplan Comprehensive Cancer Center of New York University's Medical Center.[7]

The November 7, 1992 Viewpoints article by Jerry Merkin, Publisher, *Hotel Business,* entitled "Charitable Efforts Prove We're Truly In The Hospitality Business" mentions several community relations projects that "certainly make the term 'hospitality' a living thing." See Exhibit 9-1 for details.

At the Community Relations Leaders Conference in San Antonio on February 14, 1992, Paul C. O'Brien, New England Telephone, said "a responsible corporate citizen must always be responsive to society's expectations." Mr. O'Brien added, "I view community relations as the strategic, active and ongoing participation both with and within the community to enhance not only the community but the business as well. As Willard Butcher, former chairman of Chase Manhattan Corporation, once observed, 'There is no reason that a company's altruistic and business motives cannot be in harmony.'"

As an example of New England Telephone's community activity, Mr. O'Brien told of the firm's sponsorship of the City Dance Program of the Boston Ballet. This project included support for the Boston Ballet, provided exposure to ballet for numerous inner-city children, and funded programs to bring ballet into the public schools and train minority children for dance careers with the ballet group.[8]

CHARITABLE EFFORTS PROVE WE'RE TRULY IN THE HOSPITALITY BUSINESS

There are very few businesses in this world that can boast of showing concern over the plight of people caught in dire straits, as can the lodging industry. Time and again, hoteliers have responded by giving, and not because of the positive publicity they attract. They're motivated by concern, as recent events remind us.

In the aftermath of Hurricane Andrew in Florida, hoteliers who took the lead in feeding and housing those who suffered the loss of everything through the storm. Last year, it was Best Western who led the way in feeding the Russian people facing starvation conditions in the upcoming winter. And during the holiday season of Thanksgiving and Christmas, many hoteliers open up their restaurants to feed the homeless, not for the fanfare, but because they feel it is right.

And again, during its annual membership convention last month, Best Western announced a bold move to lead the fight against homelessness and poverty, so much a problem in these tough economic times. In conjunction with Worldvision, Best Western hopes to raise substantial funds to turn the tide against this increasing problem by asking its membership to tack an extra 50 cents onto their ADR. This money would then be used as a contribution to Worldvision which is involved in the fight on poverty and homelessness.

Members have been asked to project how much their participation will generate, a step that will allow Worldvision to budget its funds in a business-like way. As spokesperson Valerie Harper explained to attendees, the funds will be channeled back to help people in the givers' areas, instead of flowing into some huge pool administered by a faceless bureaucracy.

Meanwhile, Ramada has asked its franchisees to make the holidays a nicer time for less-fortunate members of their communities by hosting a dinner for residents of retirement homes and orphanages. As President Steve

Belmonte pointed out in a memo encouraging the whole chain to participate, "with hundreds of hotels and restaurants across the United States, we can actually make a tremendous difference." The program would "touch the lives of thousands this year."

It is acts such as this, and all the other good deeds being done by the lodging industry that certainly make the term "hospitality" a living thing.

Rather than just applauding these efforts, we should all join in and help those less fortunate than we, and in return know that we have made this planet more livable for all of us.

*Hotel Business Viewpoints, Hotel Business, November 7, 1992. Copyright ICD Publications, Hotel Business, 1992.

Exhibit 9-1. Charitable Efforts Prove We're Truly in the Hospitality Business.*

Several examples of effective community relations by individual properties are provided by the winners in the American Hotel & Motel Association Gold Key Public Relations Achievement Awards program.

1989 AH&MA GOLD KEY PUBLIC RELATIONS ACHIEVEMENT AWARDS
Community Service
Individual Property Winner
Westin Hotel, Williams Center
Tulsa, Oklahoma

SENIOR HOLIDAY BALL

The Westin sponsored the Senior Holiday Ball on Christmas Day 1988 so that senior citizens in the Tulsa community would not have to celebrate this holiday alone. Nine hundred seniors enjoyed the free festivities, which included a punch and eggnog reception, a tradi-

WESTIN HOTEL, WILLIAMS CENTER, TULSA, OKLAHOMA (continued)

tional turkey dinner, dancing to the music of the 1920s and 1930s, and Christmas gifts. The Ball also sparked the holiday spirit in Tulsa's corporate community as a number of other companies and organizations volunteered their products and services to help entertain the seniors.

Publicity for the Senior Holiday Ball was excellent, with strong media interest and support prior to and after the event. Most fulfilling were the thank-you notes from the attendees. As one senior wrote, "A Christmas to truly remember—that I wasn't alone. God bless you . . . and thanks."

AH&MA GOLD KEY PUBLIC RELATIONS ACHIEVEMENT AWARDS
1991 Honorable Mention

PROPERTY: Orange Lake Country Club, Kissimmee, Florida

TITLE: Tennis with a Different Swing

AGENCY: N/A

BUDGET: N/A

SUBJECT: To host a one-of-a-kind, tennis-based, rehabilitation program for physically, mentally, or emotionally challenged people.

Conceived by the tennis professional at Orange Country Club, a vacation resort property, "Tennis with a Different Swing" uses the functions, exercises, modalities, and equipment of tennis to rehabilitate physically, mentally, or emotionally challenged people.

Using tennis, the program teaches eye-hand coordination, dexterity, balance, wheelchair motion and stability, strength, and other essential life skills.

Taking the training one step further, the Orange Country Club sponsors a team of twelve disabled play-

ORANGE LAKE COUNTRY CLUB, KISSIMMEE, FLORIDA (continued)

ers, called "OUTSPOKE'N," that travels to nearby hospitals and other facilities to conduct free public education programs on the challenges of being in a wheelchair. The team members include quadriplegics, paraplegics, an amputee, and people with burn injuries, multiple sclerosis, and spina bifida. The key message the team tries to impart is that life does not end for those confined to a wheelchair.

OUTSPOKE'N reaches a variety of people: adults, children, professionals, the challenged, and the able-bodied. They present a message that paves the way for a better understanding of people with handicaps, and employee commitment to a drug-free lifestyle.

They have even gone international. The program staff and OUTSPOKE'N flew to Mexico to educate teachers and medical personnel about the use of tennis as a rehabilitative tool. In return, the Mexican participants then visited Orange Country Club to continue their training.

The program is copyrighted, and is available from Tennis with a Different Swing free of charge.

Collateral items used:

- Tennis equipment
- Special light-weight wheelchairs

AH&MA GOLD KEY PUBLIC RELATIONS
ACHIEVEMENT AWARDS

PROPERTY: Harrah's Reno, Reno, Nevada

TITLE: Educational Support Programs

AGENCY: N/A

BUDGET: $94,339

SUBJECT: A community affairs program to support public educational systems in the areas of arts and culture, civic and community, education, and health and human services.

Recognizing their responsibility to meet their community's civic, charitable, and cultural needs, Harrah's strategically planned a public affairs program to make a definite, measurable impact on specific need areas.

Educational programs were targeted for children in kindergarten through the 12th grade to create early intervention for minority youth and youth who are at risk of dropping out of school. Harrah's recognized the need for after school programs through its involvement in both the "At-Risk" program, designed to meet the school dropout problem head-on, and the Youth Gang Task Force.

Harrah's Reno also became the first business to fully sponsor a "Latch-Key Plus" program in their community, making a commitment to fund the program for three years to provide low income, minority families with quality after school care. Available to youth, kindergarten through sixth grade, "Latch-Key Plus" provides after school recreational enrichment programs for youngsters.

Certified teachers, teachers' aides, and adult supervisors help children with organized sports and games, arts and crafts, homework assignments, cooking projects and computer science while they encourage sportsmanship and friendship in a supervised environment after school from 3:00 p.m. until 5:45 p.m. Because Harrah's underwrites the costs for "Latch-Key Plus"

HARRAH'S RENO, RENO, NEVADA (continued)

salaries, equipment, supplies, and snacks for students, parents receive quality child care for as little as 25 cents a day.

The "Latch-Key Plus" program is administered by the City of Reno Recreation Division which hires and trains staff and supervises the program. The county school district provides facilities for the program and covers the printing costs for brochures.

Harrah's was the first business to "Adopt-A-School" in their community. The "Adopt-A-School" program is designed to involve Harrah's Reno employees in high school projects and activities. The program involves more than 300 Harrah's Reno employees, from senior management to supervisors and non-salaried persons, in a multi-faceted program that includes tutoring, career lectures and "at risk" assistance for potential dropouts. Through the program the hotel has also had the opportunity to introduce students to hotel-related careers while keeping them in school.

As each new "Adopt-A-School" year begins, entertainers performing at Harrah's Reno help kick off the program by entertaining students and encouraging them to take advantage of the educational opportunities available. Harrah's employees also help teachers by "adopting" a specific class and participating in the classroom on a regular basis. These professionals have offered students tips on such topics as leadership and self-marketing during a job hunt, investments and money management, accounting, business, English as a second language, special education and ROTC.

The hotel created an "Emergency Assistance" fund for area high school students which provides needy students eye glasses, physical education uniforms, money for college entrance exam fees, or even shoes.

Harrah's joined forces with the school districts' community-based programs to set up a vocational training program at the hotel-casino. The program is designed to give students who have mental or emotional handicaps and other special needs specific training in work and social awareness.

HARRAH'S RENO, RENO, NEVADA (continued)

The objective of these programs is to directly benefit as many people as possible, and indirectly benefit the community as a whole. With a budget under $100,000, more than 150 organizations and institutions benefited from Harrah's Reno philanthropic efforts.

AH&MA GOLD KEY PUBLIC RELATIONS ACHIEVEMENT AWARDS

PROPERTY: Harvey Hotels, Plano, Texas

TITLE: N/A

AGENCY: N/A

BUDGET: N/A

SUBJECT: To participate in numerous community activities, giving the hotel a reputation for civic achievement and spirit.

The management and staff of the hotel have been involved in the life of the community on a daily basis.

Starting with the general manager, there is a concerted effort by the hotel's staff to play active roles in community and civic organizations.

Because of this involvement, the hotel participates in many civic activities working closely with the office of the mayor. The hotel management and staff donate their talent, accommodations, and meals for committee meetings and fund-raising events. Discarded items from the housekeeping department, such as soap, linens, and blankets are donated to a local homeless shelter.

The hotel management and staff work with the local school board to provide work experiences for educationally challenged teenagers. The students spend four hours a day at the hotel learning basic skills and discipline to integrate into the work force after school. Each year, the hotel hosts a banquet for these students and

HARVEY HOTELS, PLANO, TEXAS (continued)

their parents. There is also an intern program where high school students can obtain a realistic look at the hotel industry as they decide on their future careers.

Management and staff of the hotel are active on numerous non-profit boards and committees within the city. These include:

- The Mental Health Association of Collin County;
- The Substance Abuse Prevention Agency of Plano;
- The Plano Public Library Foundation;
- The Heritage Farmstead Museum;
- The Crisis Center of Collin County;
- The Collin County Women's Shelter;
- The Southern Collin County Infant Care Program;

and many others.

Almost 90 charitable, non-profit, religious, civic, fraternal, health, and educational entities have benefited from the involvement of the employees of the hotel. Some of these are:

- Ronald McDonald House;
- March of Dimes;
- The National Diabetes Association Program;
- American Red Cross blood drive;
- United Way (donated $10,000);
- Numerous Protestant, Catholic and Jewish organizations;
- Plano Independent School District;
- Collin County Crisis Center and Women's Shelter;
- Boy and Girl Scouts of America.

Collateral items used were:

- Used linens and blankets
- Discarded housekeeping items
- Donated conference rooms
- Donated banquet facilities
- Meals

AH&MA GOLD KEY PUBLIC RELATIONS ACHIEVEMENT AWARDS
1991 Honorable Mention

PROPERTY: Stouffer Pineisle Resort, Lake Lanier Islands, Georgia

TITLE: N/A

AGENCY: N/A

BUDGET: N/A

SUBJECT: To provide training to mentally challenged individuals to assist them in becoming self-supporting and to improve their quality of life.

The resort works with a non-profit organization for the mentally challenged.

In order to assure the optimum benefits to both the individuals who participate in the program and the resort, each person from the center that enters the program undergoes a rigorous period of training.

Two crews from the center—one for indoor work and one for outdoor—are utilized each day. Trainers make the individual work assignments, and instruct and assist the challenged workers until the tasks are completed.

The workers are bused to the resort each morning; they are paid by the center, which is paid by the lodge for the hours worked by the crews, minus a percentage to pay those who train the crews.

Not only must the mentally challenged individuals be trained for a specific task, they must be taught to interact with resort guests. This takes time and patience. Simple tasks that most people take for granted require hours of training for a mentally challenged person. Training of the mentally challenged workers also focuses on how they will interact with the resort's guests.

The challenged workers, once taught how to do a task, tend not to deviate from that training. The interaction with hotel guests necessitates further training. For example, once a mentally challenged person is taught that

STOUFFER PINEISLE RESORT, LAKE LANIER ISLANDS, GEORGIA (continued)

they must push the button to call an elevator, they push it even if it is already lit. If they are taught to push a cart onto the elevator once it arrives, they will not wait for people to exit the elevator before they push the cart onto the elevator.

Constant training and supervision are necessary to overcome this mindset. In time, they learn that there is no need to push the elevator button that is already lit, and to wait until people get off the elevator before they push their cart onto it.

Constant training is a huge undertaking by the resort. More time, more energy, and more money are expended to train the challenged workers. One able individual could probably do the tasks of the challenged crew. The tradeoff is in the morale for both the challenged workers and the resort staff as a whole. The resort staff take pride in the achievements and successes of the mentally challenged workers, and the staff learn how to interact with a new segment of society.

In addition, the challenged workers have learned social and job skills which they will be able to use in other job situations.

There has been very positive reaction from those guests who realize there is a mentally challenged program at the resort. Guests have been supportive, and the resort has gained a reputation as being people-oriented as well as service-oriented.

Although this book is written primarily to fit the needs of the individual hotel or restaurant, national organizations have programs that have proven to be effective and can be adapted by any hotel or restaurant owner or manager. The national programs may be nationally conceived and prepared, but are designed to be implemented locally. Some examples follow:

1. Starbucks Coffee is a national chain of coffee shops. One of its products, "The Starbucks CARE Sampler," introduces four of the chain's most popular coffees. The Starbucks CARE Sampler brochure says: "The CARE Sampler represents a gift of universal goodwill. Not only is this a wonderful introduction to four of our favorite coffees, it's a chance for you to make your own contribution to CARE above and beyond Starbucks' $100,000 ongoing annual grant. (We've priced the sampler to allow two dollars of your purchase to be passed directly on to CARE.)" Starbucks further explains that the funds will help bring clean drinking water to Indonesia and Guatemala and other benefits to Kenyan children. The tie-in is that these countries produce coffee. This program may seem a bit distant from the typical community relations program, but it does present Starbucks as a benevolent member of the community. This can help create a positive reputation for the firm.

2. Home Savings of America, a national banking organization, issued a publication called *Community* in January 1993.[9] This describes community projects its employees support with the following introduction: "Thousands of our employees volunteer countless hours each year to community groups and charitable organizations that are designed to enrich the lives of people in their community. Many of the hours spent are on the employees' own time—given out of their strong desire to help others succeed." *Community* offers numerous examples of how its employees serve their communities. Here are just a few:

- "In Fort Myers, Florida, the ACT/Abuse Counseling Treatment Center provides food, clothing, shelter, and counseling for women and children who are victims of family violence, sexual assault, or who are homeless. Savings of America's Fort Myers Branch Manager, _____ _____, donates over 30 hours each month as an on-call crisis counselor and volunteer at the Center. In addition, Home Savings of America sponsors an annual Fine Arts Auction that raises more than $100,000 for the Center."

- "The Upper Arlington Seniors Center in Ohio provides local senior citizens with a variety of recreational programs, including a men's softball team—the Silver Bears—whose members must be at least 60 years old. The team meets once a week to challenge other seniors' softball teams. Savings of America's Columbus, Ohio branch has sponsored the Silver Bears for the past four years, providing new uniforms each year and supporting the team's annual awards banquet."

- "For more than 85 years, the Abraham Lincoln Centre in Chicago, Illinois, has provided a wide range of social service activities to individuals throughout the Chicago area. The Centre offers programs aimed at early childhood development as well as special education and mental health programs for the developmentally disabled, programs for senior citizens, and counseling services for all ages." A Savings of America representative serves on the Centre's board and is active in raising money to support the programs.

3. In *Restaurant Hospitality Magazine,* April 1993, Stephen Michaelides reports that a brochure in Loews Hotels guestrooms is entitled "Doing What Comes Neighborly." Copy says: "Historically, our properties have always been responsible community members. Today, that responsibility has been given new focus. Specifically, wherever practical, all Loews hotels and resorts are now officially directed to perform the following:

- Collect all office paper and newspaper for recycling;
- Donate excess food to food banks or prepared food transfer programs;
- Exercise preference for recycled and biodegradable products;

- Support local literacy programs;
- Donate replaced items (such as linens and furniture) to local assistance organizations;
- Encourage employee participation in volunteer activities;
- In the development or renovation of (the) hotel, every effort is made to incorporate energy-and-resource-saving technologies."[10]

This program reaches out to both the customer and the community and should do much to build repeat business and aid the community at large.

4. Wendy's Old Fashioned Hamburgers joined with the National Parks and Conservation Association to help preserve and protect national parks. The concept was to introduce a new Wendy's product with a choice of premiums including a working compass, a plastic water bottle, a magnifying glass, or a nature journal featuring outdoor activities. This marketing partnership is one aspect of improving community relations and the concept could be developed by an individual unit in cooperation with a local organization whose objective is to improve the community.[11]

5. Hardee's® Food Systems, Inc. ran a public service ad with the heading:

> "HARDEE'S RESTAURANTS ACROSS THE USA SALUTE YOUNG
> PEOPLE WHO 'RISE AND SHINE' FOR THEIR COMMUNITIES.

"Each month, Hardee's will recognize school children for their efforts to give something back to their communities. The tributes are a component of Hardee's Rise and Shine for Community Service program, which is supplying elementary and middle schools across the USA with teaching material designed to educate children about the importance of community service."[12] One winner was the Stocks Elementary School in Tarboro, NC. Second graders visited earthquake-ravaged Granada Hills, California, bearing gifts of almost $4000. The money, raised through penny donations by the 530 K-2 students, was delivered to Danube Avenue Elementary School for use in rebuilding the campus.

6. New Hampshire Lodging & Restaurant Association developed a program, EDUCATION FIRST, to recognize the special needs of young workers and join educators, parents, and the teenage employees to promote and maintain a healthy balance of education and work experience. This program is based on similar programs in Indiana, Wisconsin, and Washington State developed by their restaurant associations. The manual for this program outlines how to set up a communication network between the property and other persons interested in these employees—teachers, guidance personnel, and parents. The program includes a code of ethics (in employing young people), employee checklist, employee evaluation process, recognition suggestions, sample letters, program marketing suggestions, media releases, etc. This program guideline suggests: "By adopting Education First, you establish yourself as a concerned community member, reduce employee turnover, and build positive relationship with your teen employees, parents and educators."[13]

The American Hotel & Motel Association in its Gold Key Public Relations Achievement competition over the years has recognized several small companies for their community relations programs. Several of these award-winning programs are described on the following pages:

GOLD KEY PUBLIC RELATIONS ACHIEVEMENT AWARD COMMUNITY SERVICE (Corporate) WINNER Clarion Hotels and Resorts Denver, Colorado for Clarion's for Kids

The 17 Clarion hotels embarked on a system-wide program in 1986 which called for each property to select a local charity that would benefit from the overall "Clarion's For Kids" promotion theme. Hotel employees were asked to consider the worthiness of the beneficiary and its need for funds and community attention. The staff of each property then worked with local volunteers to create a program based on the needs of the recipients. Beneficiaries included local United Way chapters, children's hospitals, poison and drug control centers, Vanished Children's Alliance, local speech and hearing schools and Big Brother/Big Sisters efforts. Staff involvement aided the local charities, but also demonstrated Clarion's concern with the communities they serve.

AH&MA GOLD KEY PUBLIC RELATIONS ACHIEVEMENT AWARDS
1991 Winner

PROPERTY: Hyatt Hotels Corporation

TITLE: The Hyatt F.O.R.C.E. (Family of Responsible and Caring Employees)

AGENCY: N/A

BUDGET: $1,987.00

SUBJECT: To participate in community life to identify areas of concern and make improvements.

The corporation wanted to make it easier for managers to get involved with community projects, to help others, and to experience the rewards of volunteerism.

The challenge was in designing a program with enough flexibility to accommodate the seasonal business demands of various hotels, along with the different volunteer needs of different communities.

Employees were informed of the program through "In TOUCH," the management newsletter, which includes photos of F.O.R.C.E. programs from around the country. At the same time, a video news magazine containing a message from the corporation president and sound bites from Hyatt employees and others involved in F.O.R.C.E. was disseminated to all Hyatt properties. The video was viewed by each of Hyatt's 55,000 employees nationwide.

Each of the corporation's 100 hotels and resorts, as well as the corporate headquarters, technical center, and worldwide reservation center, selected one local organization. Managers were given the opportunity to take at least one paid day off to volunteer with that organization.

A handbook was designed to provide all necessary guidelines to establish the individual programs. Included in the handbook were surveys to determine areas of volunteer interest, suggestions for selecting an organization, evaluation forms, and ideas for encouraging volunteers among the staff.

HYATT HOTELS CORPORATION (continued)

Some examples of the volunteer work done by F.O.R.C.E. were:

- Building a wilderness trail for the disabled;
- Helping disabled adults and children learn to ride horses as part of a physical therapy program;
- Tutoring pre-school children as part of a Head Start program;
- Assisting with Special Olympics as coaches, registrars, record keepers, and "huggers;"
- Food delivery for shut-ins;
- Formation of a "broom brigade" to sweep city streets for residents and tourists;
- Building and/or renovating low-income housing;
- Working in soup kitchens.

The success of the F.O.R.C.E. program resulted in considerable positive local and national news coverage in print and electronic media.

Continuing plans for this successful program include one paid day a quarter for management to volunteer, and opportunities for line employees to volunteer at least one day a year.

Collateral items used were:

- "How-to" books
- Employee newsletters
- News releases
- Building materials
- Tools

NOTES

1. Moore, H. Frazer, and Canfield, Bertrand R. *Public Relations Principles, Cases and Problems,* 7th ed. Richard D. Irwin, Homewood, IL, 1977, p. 9.
2. Lesly, J. Phillip (editor). *Lesly's Public Relations Handbook,* 2nd ed. Prentice Hall, Englewood, Cliffs, NJ, 1978, pp. 64, 65.
3. Lesly, *Lesly's Public Relations Handbook,* 2nd ed., p. 74.

4. Ibid., p. 75.

5. *Restaurants and Institutions,* June 1, 1993, p. 58.

6. *Successful Meetings,* March 1994, p. 23.

7. *Successful Meetings,* February 1992, p. 18.

8. Executive Speeches, *Community Relations,* October/November 1993.

9. *Community,* January 1993. Home Savings Bank, Community Outreach Department, Irwindale, California 91706.

10. "Doing What Comes Naturally." Loews Hotels. *Restaurant Hospitality,* April 1993, p. 22.

11. "Wendy's Goes Green for Success." *Restaurant Hospitality,* August 1993, p. 46.

12. "Rise and Shine," Hardee's® Restaurants. *USA Today,* March 28, 1994.

13. New Hampshire Lodging and Restaurant Association, 1994, Education First.

10

Planning to Meet Emergencies

Emergencies make bad news. And bad news may have a disastrous impact on how the public perceives your property. This, in turn, could destroy the effect of years of competent operation and drive away many past and potential guests or customers.

Crises come in many shapes and forms: accidents, earthquakes, fires, floods, murders, protest demonstrations, robberies, strikes, suicides, and others too numerous to mention.

Local, state, and federal laws and insurance costs influence your decision to create fire prevention, safety, and security programs. But chances are nobody is going to insist that you outline a crisis public-relations plan before any emergency occurs.

Remember, however, any one of the emergencies listed above is also a *public-relations emergency.* This is because any one of these events, if not managed properly, can destroy or seriously damage the most attractive image any hotel or restaurant could project to the many publics it serves or tries to attract.

The secret of minimizing the impact of any crisis on your business is contained in that time-worn Boy Scout motto: "Be Prepared."

Here is what one public-relations professional has to say on the subject.

PUBLIC RELATIONS IN AN EMERGENCY

It is most difficult to maintain good public and press relations when an accident or emergency occurs. In such situations there are persistent, seemingly unrelenting inquiries from the press, the community, business associates, government agencies, friends and relatives of employees, and other interested people. Fatigue and tension can cause short tempers and lapses in efficiency. Unless great care is taken, months of good public-relations work can be undone in a single day.

A delicate balance must be achieved between refusing to answer questions at all and giving hasty and ill-conceived responses. On the one hand, the company can be accused of withholding vital information. On the other, partial or unclear answers can result in unfavorable stories and false rumors.

However, providing good emergency services for the media can earn friends for the company regardless of the nature and scope of the problem.

Presumably the company has an excellent safety record. Thorough precautions have been taken to eliminate accidents. The company does not anticipate any serious incidents, but it must have a plan for dealing with such contingencies or it may well be considered incompetent and poorly managed, should an emergency arise.[1]

Here's how to meet any PR emergency.

To begin with, you *must* prepare *now* to meet any emergency. Only by developing in advance a strategy for working with the press in an emergency—suicide, fire, strike—can you be assured of getting the most accurate, objective coverage of it by the news media.

Regardless of which plan you finally adopt, make sure you communicate it to all employees. In addition, it's a good idea to remind them about its key elements from time to time. Don't simply let department heads file and forget it.

Here are the three basic steps that comprise a crisis press relations plan.

1. As the general manager, you should be the only spokesperson in times of crisis or emergency. Make sure that your department heads or supervisors tell employees—and then remind them occasionally—that they are not to talk to reporters during emergencies but should refer all inquiries to you or your publicity coordinator, who will then contact you. Therefore, someone on the staff must know how to reach you at all times—day or night. More and more today, reporters try to find people whom the crisis affects or who actually witnessed the accident or fire. Accordingly, you may lose control of the situation anyway. But do everything in your power to make sure that none of your employees except the spokesperson is interviewed.
2. Before responding to questions from the media, determine quickly and accurately the facts surrounding the crisis situation.
3. Once you know the story is out, initiate contact with the news media. Don't wait for them to call you. This way, you ensure that they get accurate information and will reflect your cooperation in their reporting.

IMPORTANT: In situations involving serious injury or death, names of those killed or injured must not be released to the news media until next of kin has been notified.

Be prepared to meet the needs of the media quickly. Make certain all employees are alerted to admit to the property reporters with proper credentials. If there has been a fire, explosion, or other disaster, however, news media people should not be allowed to wander around the premises alone (after the situation is under control). "Deputize" staff members to escort them through the property once its structural integrity has been assured.

Provide telephone operators with a brief message to read to callers who may flood the hotel/motel switchboard. But be sure to *caution them against answering questions of any kind.* All inquiries should be referred to the hotel or restaurant spokesperson. If necessary, provide reporters with special telephone facilities to be used by them only.

If members of the press wish to interview guests, it's usually best, when possible, to designate an out-of-the-way area where the TV people can get good camera angles.

WHAT THE MEDIA WILL WANT TO KNOW

Most of the questions reporters will ask in these situations are the basic Who, What, Where, When, Why, and How. It's fairly simple to be prepared beforehand, if you anticipate their queries. If you don't know an answer, say so. Never—especially in emergencies—say "No comment" and let it go at that. Always explain why you cannot comment. For example, "The police department is still investigating." Simply tell the reporters you'll try to get the answer, if possible, and that you will get back to them.

The following questions are typical of those the media may ask after an emergency involving injury or death:

- What caused the accident, injury, or fatality?
- Name, age, job title, and home address of person(s) hurt or killed. (*IMPORTANT:* this information should not be released until next of kin is notified.)
- When did the incident, injury, or fatality occur?
- Where did it happen?
- How (or why) did it happen? Answer only with facts that are easily verifiable. *Never speculate.* Politely refuse media requests for a statement of probable cause(s).

TRY TO PUT A POSITIVE SLANT ON THE NEWS

At such times, it's perfectly reasonable to indicate that the cause of the disaster is "under investigation." If there has been a death or deaths, refer media to the police department. Try, where appropriate, to focus the attention of reporters on the diligent efforts of management or employees to cope with the emergency, for example, rescue or care of the injured and reduced damages.

You might give the names of employees who helped by

- alerting guests to the danger;
- leading guests to safety;
- rescuing or caring for the injured;
- reducing damage or loss of life in any other way.

Questions the media may ask concerning explosions, fires, or natural disasters are slightly different. For example:

- What caused the explosion or fire? This question should be referred to the fire department spokesperson.
- How much damage was done? Avoid any dollar estimate, even a "ball park figure." If you're wrong, you'll regret seeing this number in print or hearing it on the news. The extent of damage may be indicated only in a general way.
- Is the damage covered by insurance? Unless legal problems are involved, give a straightforward answer. If the property is insured, the media can be told truthfully that the dollar amount of damage will be determined by insurance investigators.

Suicides, bombings, and irrational actions of deranged people may happen on rare occasions in a hotel or motel. Should any of these take place at your property, immediately contact your legal counsel to prepare statements for release to the press. It is appropriate for the spokesperson to request that the name of the property not be mentioned by the media because research suggests that when other disturbed persons learn of the tragedy they are frequently drawn to the same place to commit similar acts. Ask that the media refer to the property as "a downtown hotel" or a "Route 66 Inn," for example.

DEALING WITH GROUP DISTURBANCES

Problems of this type might include picketing or aggressive activity by:

- organizations critical of the property's hiring or employment policies; or
- consumer groups taking issue with one of more of the property's services.

If the protesting group is in non-public rooms or property, you have a legal right to ask the members to leave. Again, legal counsel should be sought to protect your rights. If the group is not actually on your property, you should handle relations with the media in the same manner as previously described (i.e., appointing a spokesperson, preparing a response with advice of legal counsel, and holding a news conference if so advised).

Bad news such as this can be aggravated when the group sponsoring the activity informs the media ahead of time of its intentions. This means reporters, television cameras, and photographers may be on the scene before you're even aware of what is happening.

Once you learn of the situation, you should prepare a media statement. It should be approved by legal counsel, if possible, and should be brief, factual, and as objective as possible. Also, notify the police.

If the group disturbance is well organized and members have contacted the media in advance, you can be certain that they have prepared their own written information for release to the media. You are justified in asking for a copy of this material—either from the media or the group itself. This will help you in preparing your own statement. If you cannot obtain this information in written form or orally, it is reasonable for you to respond to media questions by saying you cannot comment on something about which you know nothing.

MAINTAINING GOOD PUBLIC RELATIONS
DURING A STRIKE

There are two schools of thought when it comes to handling media inquiries during a strike. One holds that property and union representatives should agree to not issuing public statements while negotiations are being conducted. The other maintains that the lines of public communication be kept open.

If you adopt the first position, merely tell the media that neither management nor the union will discuss the situation until contract negotiations are ended.

If you adopt the second procedure, prepare a statement outlining management's position on the issue(s) in dispute. It is wise to clear this with your legal counsel before releasing it.

Legal counsel may advise the property not to deal with the press during a period of labor problems. Therefore, as soon as any labor problems arise, you should consult counsel to establish your policy of media relations in the event of a subsequent strike.

If a property is confronted with a strike threat, it is advisable to immediately contact an expert public relations firm in addition to legal counsel. Because the period of a strike is unpredictable, such expert opinion is vital. Time is of the essence because labor groups have extensive experience in media relations, and the property must act quickly and efficiently to counter labor press releases.

Be willing to talk to the media during this time. They will be interested in management's point of view, so be accessible. Be factual; do not allow emotions to cloud your remarks. Know the specific terms of disagreement. You'll need such information as names of union leaders, the local number and name of the parent union, reasons given by the strikers for walking out, and the number of workers involved. Also, be prepared to state which parts of your property will continue to operate during the strike.

It's important to maintain good public relations all the time because, during a strike, editorial content and the slant of the news will reflect how your property has been viewed by the community in the past.

For additional information about dealing with the media during periods of crisis, we suggest you read *Crisis Communications,* published by the Communications Department of the American Hotel and Motel Association.[2]

Just how important is a public-relations plan to deal with emergencies? When a major hotel fire kills or injures one or more of your guests or an employee or guest is the victim of food poisoning, the hotel or restaurant is *placed on trial* in the press and in the public mind *long* before juries get around to finding legal fault. How management reacts in this period can mean the difference between a temporary loss of public good will and the permanent loss of a sizable chunk of your room and food sales.

We hope it will never be necessary for any reader to use the techniques enumerated in the Crisis PR Plan (Exhibit 10-1) and a few others we're going to cite. But that's not a very realistic thing to hope for. If you count all the hotel and restaurant disasters—large and small—that occur in one year, some of you can expect to need to use at least a few of these techniques at some time in the future.

It's worth recalling that although *everybody* suffers when something serious goes wrong, it's the general manager who failed to prepare who always suffers the most.

A hotel walkway collapses, six people die in a fire, the controversial CEO of a multinational company is taken hostage in his hotel suite: such events strike dread among management and top executives.

What should you do when the unthinkable happens? By this, of course, we mean *after* you have called the police or sounded the fire alarm, learned what happened, and organized your staff to assist the police or fire officers.

Your first job is to learn what happened, and take whatever corrective action you can immediately; in the event of a fire or other life-threatening emergency, evacuate your guests and employees in as orderly a manner as possible.

If your office or any other office or room with a phone is usable, you should set up a command post. Then, decide what you want your employees to do and, using your department heads and supervisors, get the word to all of them as soon as possible.

A CRISIS PUBLIC-RELATIONS PLAN

Following are excerpts from an actual crisis public-relations plan developed for a hotel management company. [A number of alterations to the original plan were suggested by one of the authors in remarks delivered to a meeting of company managers. These changes are incorporated in the composite plan.]

Maintaining good public relations is most difficult during a crisis or emergency. Public relations planning is essential, so that if an emergency arises, inquiries from the news media, guests, friends and relatives can be handled effectively. Although we cannot turn a disaster around, we can assist in making sure facts presented to the public are accurate and as positive as possible, given the situation. Therefore, you should prepare action plans to defuse disaster before it happens.

WHAT CONSTITUTES AN EMERGENCY?

An emergency is any situation or event that may be interpreted in a manner harmful to the hotel or restaurant that is subject to coverage by the news media in a way that's not in the interests of the hotel or (name of company).

PLANNING FOR CRISIS COMMUNICATION

First, identify a single spokesman, preferably you, the general manager. As forcefully as possible, direct all other employees to refrain from commenting publicly in a crisis.

BUILD A POTENTIAL DISASTER LIST

Here are just a few examples: fire, explosion, flood, hurricane, suicide, strike, hostage situation, food poisoning, serious accident. I'm sure you can think of others. Every time you hear or read about a disaster that happened to another hotel, add it to your list. Decide whether it could happen to your hotel, and if it could, plan for it.

Distribute and post in the employees' breakroom the chain of command—the names and phone numbers of whom to report to when an emergency occurs.

GUIDE FOR HANDLING THE NEWS MEDIA DURING EMERGENCIES

Never say anything "off the record." The standard rule is, "If you don't want to see it in print or on the TV or radio, don't say it!"

Let reporters know that you may withhold information that violates an individual's right to privacy or that jeopardizes your organization's legal rights.

As soon as possible, *prepare a company statement for the press,* acknowledging an accident has occurred and that steps to combat and control are being taken. You may wish to have your lawyer prepare or review this.

1. Speed in reply to a question is important. All reporters have deadlines to meet. True, but make sure you have all the facts first.
2. Keep cool. If a reporter loses his temper, remember he has deadlines to meet. Try to cooperate to the extent possible.
3. Never say "no comment" and let it go at that. For example, if you cannot comment on the cause of a disaster because it is under investigation, it is perfectly appropriate to say so.
4. Make it as easy as possible for the reporter. Any attempt at obstacles may make the reporter work harder to uncover the real story. Although you can't tell the reporter everything, tell as much as possible.
5. When it becomes necessary to admit a fact already known to the press, be sure confirmation is limited only to definite information that will not change. Never speculate as to the cause of accidents, amount of damage, responsibility, possible down-time, lay-offs, etc.

FACTS DESIRED—BUT NOT DESIRABLE TO GIVE

1. *Speculate* on *NOTHING!*
2. What caused the incident? Let someone else release this. Chances are the story will die before the report is completed.
3. Specific damage estimated as well as what was destroyed.

HANDLING THE EMERGENCY

1. The general manager will maintain contact with reporters, making sure they stay in approved locations while on hotel property and providing information to them as quickly as possible.
2. The responsibility of giving facts to the press and public rests with the general manager or someone from (name of company).
3. Maintain close contact with individual members of the media. They might be able to tell you things you do not already know. This also prevents the flow of false information.
4. Log all facts released, including the times. This will avoid duplication and conflicting reports should new developments change facts.
5. Never ask to see a reporter's story. If you feel the reporter may be misinformed, check back on the point to be sure.
6. There's seldom a reason why you should not be quoted by name.
7. Never argue with a reporter about the value of a story.
8. Any information given to one source should be given to all.
9. Never refuse to reveal information without an explanation.
10. Always know to whom you are talking.
11. Never falsify, color, or slant your answers. A reporter can see it coming and nothing sets the journalist off faster than this.

12. Be cautious of photographs. Although you have no control of photos taken outside your property, you have the right to control photos taken within the hotel.
13. Be sure there is the least possible delay between the time you get information and when you give it to the media.
14. Have safety, labor, and employee records available for your reference.
15. If damage must be estimated for the press, confine your statement to a general description of what was destroyed.
16. Always accentuate the positive if you possibly can. As facts become known, clear them and give them to the news media.
17. *DO NOT* release the names of victims until you know for certain that the families involved have been notified. Tell reporters the name(s) of victim(s) will not be released pending notification of next of kin. Then follow up to see that they get these names as soon as possible.

QUESTIONS OFTEN ASKED

1. Number of deaths.
2. Number of injuries.
3. Damage (Fire chief will give estimate in dollars. Give yours in GENERAL TERMS of what was destroyed as soon as you know).
4. What burned or collapsed?
5. Time.
6. Location within property.
7. Names of dead and injured, following notification of relatives.
8. Their addresses, ages, and how long with company, as well as occupation.
9. How many people employed?

A representative should coordinate a follow-up news release after the height of the emergency has passed, to present the company in as positive a light as possible.

Depending on the nature of the emergency, possible topics include

1. What has been done to prevent recurrence of this type of emergency?
2. What are the plans for reconstruction?
3. What has been done to express gratitude to the community for its help?
4. What has been done to help employees?
5. Make sure, where appropriate, that employees are recognized for their help in saving lives, deterring the spread of fire, etc.

Exhibit 10-1. A Crisis Public-Relations Plan.

In case an evacuation is needed, employees should be pre-assigned to strategic locations, at stairwells and near exit doors, with flashlights. Another part of your advance planning, of course, sould be to have several stockpiles of flashlights (equipped with fresh batteries) and candles spotted throughout the hotel or restaurant.

Then, it's your job to contact the media, disclose the story, put it into context, tell your side, and get it over with. If they get all the information they need from you, quickly, chances are it will all appear in one story or newscast—and be over with. If the reporters have to pry it out of you or seek out other sources, this usually takes time. And that often means that bits of information will appear in two or more news articles or broadcasts, spaced out over a period of several days. Since there are more stories or newscasts, more people will see or hear the bad news about your hotel or restaurant.

Years ago, a company's first response to an emergency was to say little or nothing. But television and vast improvements in other communications technology changed all that.

Take the case of an airplane crash. Before the advent of on-the-scene TV news coverage, some airlines would dispatch crews of workmen to the scene in the hopes of being able to paint out the airline's name, logo, or other identifying marks before the newspaper photographers or newsreel cameramen showed up. The basic idea was to prevent or at least slow down the dissemination of bad news.

Not any more. Now the trend is in the opposite direction. This can be attributed to the development of local, regional TV news coverage and the use of jets, helicopters, and high-speed vans to ferry TV camera people, newspaper photographers, and television, radio, and TV reporters to the scene of any disastrous accident or other crisis. The emphasis now is on immediate disclosure of all that is *known.*

Television wields tremendous influence over the way viewers perceive events, individuals, businesses, governments, and other institutions. And emergencies are no exception. Poor or sloppy handling of any emergency can seriously affect how the public perceives your establishment. We have advised you to get the news out fast. But don't jump the gun. It's a good idea to withhold comment until all the facts are in.

In the meantime, if any part of your building is still usable, it's advisable to set up a press room or media center and extend full cooperation to the press. If not, you may have to designate a spot out of doors or in a nearby building. Ideally, the press room should contain chairs, tables, telephones, typewriters, a fax machine, and ample supplies of paper, pencils, memo pads, and coffee, and, of course, if available, press kits giving background information on the hotel.

Here's another suggestion: In preparing the PR *plan* for dealing with emergencies at your hotel you may want to consult with your attorney. What's more, you should consider whether your lawyer should aid in preparing any statement to the media. The idea behind this is to ensure that you do not jeopardize any of your legal rights or the outcome of possible lawsuits.

Chapter 3 advised you to get to know the media and suggested how best to do this. Keep in mind that how you deal with an emergency or disaster can make or break your hotel. An unfavorable news story often makes people think twice about staying at a particular lodging establishment.

However, correct PR procedures can help alleviate a lot of the pain. A grease fire that starts in one of your range exhaust hoods can result in a screaming newspaper headline on page one or three that *names* your hotel. Or, it can produce a short item on page 18. What determines the outcome, you may well ask? If a reporter knows and likes you, he'll often write "a local hotel" without even mentioning your hotel or restaurant's name. Which means it's important for you, as the general manager, to be *well acquainted* with the reporters and editors in your town.

This is so important that it could well be your first step in devising your own PR plan for dealing with emergencies. You or whomever you appoint to serve as your contact with the news media should get to know the media right now—before any crisis erupts.

Using one or more of the ideas set forth in the sample plan and in the rest of this chapter, you can tailor a PR plan to help you cope with practically any kind of disaster. Your plan could well be in the form of a check list or a series of queries, so that you and your key people can make sure, at a glance, that you have observed all of the "rules and regulations."

Simply having a plan isn't enough. Once it's in place, it's up to you, as the general manager, to see that your staff is trained to deal with emergencies. How they perform during a fire, flood, or other crisis will determine, at least in part, how people will perceive your hotel.

At a time like this you will be deeply concerned about the safety of your guests or customers and employees as well as for the reputation of your establishment. For these reasons you will want to arrange *now* for a number of your employees to be trained in first aid and to take whatever emergency training courses your local police and fire departments recommend.

From a PR standpoint, of course, your people need to be reminded frequently, during staff meetings and in memos, that during emergencies only the general manager or his or her representative should speak to the press.

One final piece of advice: During an emergency, if you do not *manage* your own news event, someone else is sure to *mismanage* it for you.

One of the important categories in AH&MA's Gold Key Public Relations Achievement Awards program is Crisis Public Relations.

Synopses and excerpts from some of these prize-winning entries are given below.

First place in Crisis Public Relations in the 1982 program was won by Marriott Hotels, which earned favorable publicity and recognition as a fine corporate citizen after a shocking tragedy.

Two Marriott Hotels near Washington, D.C. were among the closest to the site of the Air Florida Flight 90 crash. Both hotels and the company's public-relations department responded to the immediate needs of police, rescue workers, families of passengers, the airline, government officials, and the media by providing shelter, food, and communications facilities during the crisis.

In the Crisis Public Relations category, first place in the 1981 competition went to the Hyatt on Union Square, San Francisco, CA, for its handling of an "emergency" public-relations program during a one-month strike against San Francisco's major hotels by the Culinary Union. The Hyatt, along with the 37 other hotels struck, faced additional problems, aside from those presented by the strike itself. It was directed not to make any statements regarding the strike and all press material and statements were to be issued by the Hotel Employers Association (HEA) and its public-relations firm.

The Hyatt management soon realized the HEA and its PR firm were doing little or nothing to portray the hotels' point of view in the dispute. It had to reach the media on its own.

When the hotel knew the strike was imminent, although it had not been called officially, it opened up all its "channels of communication," and managed to place stories with local broadcast media on the "family" atmosphere enjoyed by the

Hyatt Hotel and its employees. Five days into the strike the Hyatt's management decided to give its PR and Advertising Director Sandie Wernick permission to get the hotel's side of the dispute covered in the press.

Wernick lived in the hotel during the one-month strike, established contact with the city's media, and slowly, but surely, saw to it that the hotel's view of the issues reached the public. Wernick's efforts and availability to the press paid off: The initial negative attitude toward hotel management turned to a more positive, and certainly more objective, evaluation of the issues during the strike and the honesty and accessibility of both the management and public relations staff during a difficult time were remembered and appreciated after the strike was settled.

What happens when a brand new telephone system serving over 1800 guest rooms in The Waldorf-Astoria breaks down the moment it's first turned on? One of New York's poshest hotels becomes The Waldorf-Hysteria. For 15 hours, the hotel was forced to revert to nineteenth-century communications, with staff members hand-delivering messages to guests who could call out but could not receive incoming calls. To compound the problem, room numbers had been changed during the night to conform with the new system. Some guests, after an evening of revelry, couldn't find their rooms.

Public relations veteran Frances Borden kept cool throughout. "There were two important stories to be told (to the media)," she said. "The Waldorf was the injured party because the telephone company's equipment had not lived up to promises; and the staff of The Waldorf was heroic . . . coming in to work on their day off, answering individual emergency phones and delivering messages on foot to guests in a 42-story building covering a New York City square block."

The judges were unanimous in awarding The Waldorf-Astoria first place in the 1980 awards program's Crisis Public Relations category. While the media had a field day capitalizing on the black humor of the situation, The Waldorf impressed the world with its ability to handle a difficult situation with aplomb.

To prepare general managers and public relations people to handle emergencies effectively, a Crisis Communications Policy was written by the public-relations department of Carnival Hotels and Casinos. It appears as Exhibit 10-2.

This policy was developed as part of the company's Public Relations Manual for Sales Managers. Excerpts from other sections of the manual comprise Exhibit 11-1 in Chapter 11.

(This is a segment of the Public Relations Manual for Sales Managers prepared by the public relations department of Carnival Hotels and Casinos (CHC). The company owns or manages some 60 hotels in the United States, the Caribbean, and Latin America. These run the gamut from airport hotels to conference centers, limited service properties, and five-star resorts. The manual was prepared for the general managers and sales directors of the hotels, many of whom do not have an in-house public-relations person or retain a public-relations agency.)*

CRISIS COMMUNICATIONS POLICY

In the event of a crisis or occurrence that results in or may result in contact or coverage by the media, it is Carnival Hotels and Casinos' policy that preparation for and contact be made with the corporate public relations department as soon as reasonably possible.

I. WHEN TO COMMUNICATE

Immediately upon learning of a crisis situation, notify your Regional Vice President/Operations and the Corporate Public Relations Director. Do not talk to anyone, especially the media, until a unified mission statement and action plan have been developed and a spokesperson selected.

After a crisis situation has occurred, perferably within one hour, a carefully prepared press statement should be drafted with details that have been gathered and confirmed. Details should cover the basics: who, what, when, where, why, and how.

If people have been injured or killed, the names of the victims should not be released. Advance coordination with the local and regional hospital administrations regarding this policy is advised. Particularly, each should be requested orally and in writing not to release information with reference to accident/crisis circumstances to the media.

* Reprinted courtesy of Carnival Hotels & Casinos.

Key timetable elements of a crisis situation requiring announcement to the press:

1. Immediately upon hearing of a crisis, contact your Regional Vice President/Operations and the corporate Director of Public Relations to review the situation and develop a mission statement and plan of action.
2. After assessment of the situation, prepare a press statement (i.e., number of people injured/killed/affected and property damage). Be extremely accurate and careful of details given out—NEVER, NEVER speculate.
3. Offer progress reports of new details and status report of activities undertaken to alleviate the problem.
4. Issue a final statement announcing the situation is under control and listing measures taken to avoid repetition of the problem.

II. CONTROLLING COMMUNICATIONS

Key people, such as switchboard operators, security guards, safety personnel, receptionists, secretaries, and managers, should have advance instructions about where and to whom they should direct all calls requesting information. They should also be instructed not to answer any questions personally.

III. SELECTING A DESIGNATED SPOKESPERSON

It is up to the corporate public relations director, in consultation with appropriate officers in the Hospitality Group, to determine whether the problem is on a scale that would warrant the corporate public relations officer to serve as spokesperson during the crisis.

If someone from the hotel will serve as spokesperson, determine in advance who that person will be. Consult the following persons in the order listed below to determine the appropriate spokesperson for the property.

General Manager
Corporate Public Relations Director
Regional Vice President/Operations

By always having *only one* key spokesperson responsible during any given crisis situation, the property can be certain that the information given out will be consistent, accurate, and sensitive to corporate, property, and public concerns.

It is preferable to have top property management respond to the press. An image of being in control of the situation creates public confidence.

A. SPECIALIZED SPOKESPERSONS:

1. For detailed technical situations a technical expert should be designated and included in the development of information distributed to the public and media.

2. Appropriate law enforcement and/or fire department officials should be notified immediately, where applicable.

IV. WHAT AND HOW TO COMMUNICATE

All written and oral statements should be prepared in cooperation with and receive approval by the corporate public relations director.

Be honest and straightforward with the press. If they don't get the information from your spokesperson, they will get it from someone else. More than likely, that information will be distorted, inaccurate, and much more damaging than the truth. Sufficient, factual dissemination of information will help the property avoid rumors and false information.

The cause and details can't always be determined immediately. In such cases it is perfectly all right to say, "The cause of the _____ is not yet determined" or "I don't have that information yet, but I will release the facts the moment they are available."

NOTE: The press should only be allowed on the scene if it is safe, authorized by the authorities having jurisdiction where applicable, and Carnival Hotels and Casinos headquarters, and they are escorted by assigned and competent property management personnel. *It is im-*

portant, however, for all employees to be aware that they are not to discuss the situation with anyone, especially the press, even if asked questions.

Releasing information to the press can take several forms:

1. Written news releases (messengered or hand-carried to press offices).
2. Oral announcements by property management (a written copy of the statement should be released at the same time to avoid misquotes).
3. Depending on the situation, fact sheets, spot radio announcements, telephone hotlines, bulletin board announcements, and letters to employees may be necessary.

Once the crisis is over, a follow-up letter of assurance to employees, community officials, and others affected by the situation will help maintain positive rapport and create confidence in the company among employees and the news media.

V. DOS AND DON'TS

✔ **Do** take your time and prepare your statements before responding to the media.
✔ **Do** indicate that the property is willing to cooperate with the press by trying to provide the most up-to-date and accurate information while trying to meet its deadlines.
✔ **Do** attempt to correct misleading statements you believe are being made by persons outside the property.
✔ **Do** monitor the news coverage and make a courteous effort to bring inaccurate information to the attention of the media.
✔ **Do** accentuate existing and factual positive aspects: the property's safety record, plans for rebuilding, continuing precautions, acts of heroism, concern for

employees, etc., but do so without glossing over the negative aspects. Remain positive but sincere.

✔ **Don't** rush to respond to the media. Make sure you have your facts straight.

✔ **Don't** attempt to blame anyone for anything.

✔ **Don't** EVER speculate on anything.

✔ **Don't** release information on people involved. Respect their right to privacy.

✔ **Don't** release damage or cost estimates without confirming their accuracy and receiving prior approval from corporate public relations.

✔ **Don't** *make "off the record" statements to the press. In a crisis situation, no statement is "off the record."*

✔ **Don't** play favorites with the media. Give the same information to all.

✔ **Don't** *"Ad-Lib": stick to a prepared statement where possible.* Be sure to keep a written list of any responses to the media not included in the prepared statement. This will ensure that you are providing the identical information and answer to all members of the news media.

✔ **Don't** repeat negative or inflammatory words used by a reporter. It could end up as part of your quote.

✔ **Don't** demonstrate a great deal of emotion during interviews, which might convey panic, particularly on TV. It is preferable to do TV interviews off camera. Above all, don't cover up, mislead, or lie to the press.

VI. EMPLOYEE PROGRAMS

If a particular crisis involves an employee death, we urge the property to consider conducting a memorial service for employees. This will demonstrate management's concern and empathy for the victim's family and friends. Group counseling for employees should also be considered, depending on the nature of the crisis.

VII. CONCLUSION

The implementation of the procedures outlined herein will ensure the speedy dissemination of accurate information to the press during any emergency. However, precautions should be taken in advance to eliminate the need to utliize these procedures.

Planning a crisis avoidance program is a five-step process:

1. Determine where potential problems exist.
2. Define them.
3. Select solutions.
4. Plan their implementation.
5. Monitor progress toward that goal.

The Carnival Hotels and Casinos public relations department is available to assist in developing public relations plans and procedures to minimize adverse publicity in the event of a crisis.

Exhibit 10-2. Crisis Communications Policy.

NOTES

1. Culligan, Matthew J., and Green, Dolph. *Getting Back to the Basics of Public Relations and Publicity.* Crown Publishing, New York, 1982, p. 53.
2. Reprinted with permission from *PROTECT YOUR IMAGE: Effective Media Relations for the Lodging Industry.* Copyright 12/14/87 by the Educational Institute of the American Hotel & Motel Association, P.O. Box 1240, East Lansing, MI 48826.

11

Learning from the Experts: Ideas You Can Use

Amateurs can learn from professionals in any field. With this in mind, the authors asked a number of hotel companies with public-relations agencies or departments a series of questions to determine their PR goals and how they attempt to achieve them. Following is a summary of the replies from representatives of three companies.

The first question asked the companies to describe the primary goals of their PR department.

Forte Hotels, Inc. says it conducts its public-relations activities on two tiers. Functions on the first or industry level are aimed at increasing awareness of Forte among hospitality industry professionals and potential franchisees. This is accomplished by announcing new franchise development offices, personnel changes, new financing programs, etc. Activities on the second or consumer level have as their chief goals increasing brand name awareness and loyalty among guests and potential guests. To do this, Forte publicizes Travelodge's value-added promotions and frequent guest programs.

Red Roof Inns has as its primary PR goals "putting the (chain's) best foot forward" and positioning the company "as a leader in lodging hospitality."

The chief objective of Carnival Hotels & Casinos' corporate public relations department

> is to disseminate (to selected media) factual information about our company and its operations in a timely manner. . . . We also serve as the central clearing point for all media inquiries and are charged with maintaining a uniform corporate message in all communications from every department/property/employee to the public.

The second question involved the responsibilities and duties of the PR department.

Forte says its PR responsibilities and duties are to oversee all communication with the media, within the corporation, to its properties and with Forte Hotels, Inc.'s parent company, London-based Forte Plc.

These five responsibilities and duties are listed by Red Roof Inns:

- Writing and editing company and guest publications
- Overseeing all media relations
- Coordinating all grand opening activities
- Managing crisis communications
- Orchestrating community relations

Carnival reports its PR department

> is responsible for handling all corporate communications as well as providing ongoing public relations counsel and assistance to each division of the company and the hotels and casinos we manage. To ensure a unified message for the company and all of its hotel and casino properties, the public relations department is responsible for writing and distributing all corporate news releases and newsletters, arranging press conferences and speaking engagements for corporate spokespersons, coordinating appropriate interviews for key executives as well as referring requests from editors and writers for information on industry trends, system-wide

gaming or travel promotions, family travel, group or FIT packages and rates, restaurants and recipes, individual site reviews and press trips. We are also available to offer guidance and assistance on major events at our hotels and casinos, such as grand openings, renovations, re-naming, new executive staff announcements, etc.

"Organizationally, where does your public-relations activity fit?" was the third question. The three firms responded as follows:

Forte:

> Public relations cannot be restricted to an individual category, and at the unit level, more than any other, public relations is integrated into every discipline that the manager/operator handles. For example, it is possible that the person who is on a sales call to the property may also be an excellent lead for future business to the individual property.

Red Roof:

> Public relations has become a much more valued function in our company over the past few years. Senior management better understands how important this role is to the success of our company.

Carnival:

> The corporate public relations department is part of the marketing department and consists of the director of public relations, assistant director of public relations and PR/advertising assistant. As director of public relations I report to the senior vice president/marketing, however, I also report directly to the chairman and/or presidents of the hospitality and gaming divisions of the company on certain projects.

A close relationship between public relations and marketing is indicated by the replies from all three companies to this question: "Describe the responsibility/organizational relationship between public relations and the sales and marketing function."

Carnival puts it this way:

> The marketing department consists of regional sales and marketing directors, reservations, public relations and advertising. The director of public relations attends all marketing meetings and interacts daily with all members of the marketing team on various projects. Requests for public relations assistance/support from the properties are channeled through the regional directors of marketing to the director of public relations who then decides on the appropriate action to be taken and involves the necessary personnel and/or agency support.

According to Forte:

> Very few companies can afford what used to be termed "public relations" and any activity that requires funding must show a return on the investment which is why we term our activity "marketing communications." In our definition, marketing communications is driven by marketing and sales, and utilizes typical and traditional public relations tactics to support sales and marketing initiatives.

Red Roof says, simply:

> The public relations role falls under the marketing umbrella. Public relations works very closely with marketing and sales to help deliver the best message to our various audiences.

Next, the person in charge of PR for each company was asked, "Do you act as spokesperson for your company? If not, who is the spokesperson or do you share the responsibility? (If shared, with whom?)"

Red Roof:

> In my position of public relations coordinator, I am responsible for acting as company spokesperson.

Forte:

> [The] Director of Communication at Forte Hotels serves as the company spokesperson on a daily basis. For scheduled interviews,

the executive who oversees that particular subject (i.e., marketing, franchise development) will serve as the spokesperson.

Carnival:

> The official spokesperson for our company are the chairman and CEO, president of the hospitality group, and president of the gaming group. Depending on the media's topic and spokesperson availability, I channel the interview request to the appropriate person with as much background information on the topic and reporter as possible. All employees at both the corporate office and the properties have been instructed through our Media Relations Guidelines to forward all media requests for corporate information to me or someone in my office for evaluation. This allows us the opportunity to determine who should handle the call and what message should be conveyed, and how to follow up, if necessary. The appropriate spokesperson for each of our properties is usually the General Manager or whomever is in charge of the operation. This spokesperson is available to the media to discuss topics directly related to that particular operation and should refer any additional questions on the parent company to me.

All three companies indicated they have public relations manuals or plans and written crisis/emergency plans that serve as guides to their PR people and others in the organizations.

Carnival asks its properties for their "best" public relations stories quarterly. Two of its PR Idea Exchange entries appeared in Chapters 7 and 9.

To improve community relations, Red Roof encourages inns to work with local elementary schools to "host" room cleaning seminars. Concerning special events, the company reports continued success in opening new Red Roof Inns and teaming with local Chambers of Commerce to "introduce our business."

Our final question: "What advice can you give to the unit manager or independent operator who does not have public-relations staff or home office public-relations support?"

Carnival offers these suggestions:

> It is imperative to train staff to be "public relations experts" with every person they meet. They should know about the hotel's

features, food and beverage outlets, special packages and promotions, etc. They should wear smiles on their faces and have a pleasant, helpful attitude with everyone—both on and off the job. Telephone operators and reservations agents have a special opportunity to "spread the word" about the hotel by offering helpful information to callers and "selling" additional features to potential guests. There is no better PR than word-of-mouth recommendations from pleased guests!

Hotels also have an important PR opportunity within their communities. Creating special promotions for local charities, participating in chamber of commerce or convention and visitors bureau (CVB) events, sponsoring local athletic teams, etc. all garner additional publicity for the property and may have the added benefit of driving new business into the hotel.

Creating a link with the PR person/department of your local CVB and/or governmental division of tourism office can be especially productive. Often these offices are in touch with local and national media and need partnership with local business to respond to media requests and/or host journalists visiting the area.

Guidance from Forte consists of the following:

Utilize public relations in everything you do and be clever with promotions and media coverage will follow. Also, set your property apart and be aware of the competition. What makes it different? Take advantage of anything beneficial that occurs at your property and use it to your advantage. It is also essential to maintain regular contact with the media and be available to them at all times. If a crisis occurs at your property, establish one person as the media contact and develop a statement to be distributed to the entire staff should a reporter attempt to contact them.

This succinct answer comes from Red Roof:

Read the papers to see how other companies are handling public relations situations. Also, work to improve your writing and always proof, proof, proof.

Exhibit 11-1 includes selected excerpts from a Public Relations Manual developed by the public relations department of Carnival Hotels and Casinos. A segment of this manual, Crisis Communications Policy, appears as Exhibit 10-2.

PUBLIC RELATIONS MANUAL
FOR SALES MANAGERS

ON-SITE PUBLIC RELATIONS COORDINATOR/MANAGER
JOB DESCRIPTION

The Public Relations Coordinator/Manager will function under the supervision of Carnicon's corporate public relations director and will serve as a public relations liaison for their particular property with Carnicon's corporate public relations department. Responsibilities include

- Maintaining regular contact with local and regional print and broadcast media;
- Distributing news releases to appropriate local media on appropriate special events, personnel announcements, and newsworthy programs;
- Distributing press kits to appropriate local and visiting journalists;
- Updating press kits with new materials prepared and approved by headquarters;
- Reading local and regional media and forwarding articles on Carnicon or your property to the corporate director of public relations on a timely basis;
- Assisting with coordination of press trips and/or individual site reviews of your property;
- Identifying appropriate media interviews or promotional opportunities;
- Creating and implementing special events; and
- Maintaining regular contact with key travel partners who may assist in press trips, site reviews, promotions, special events, etc.
- Maintaining Carnicon's standards of Public Relations activities at the hotel level.

WHAT IS PUBLIC RELATIONS?

I. NEWS IS WHAT'S HAPPENING,
      NAMES MEANS NEWS,
            NEWS MEANS RECOGNITION,
                  RECOGNITION MEANS PRESTIGE . . .

Opportunities are everywhere for Carnicon-managed resorts and casinos to be recognized in magazines, newspapers, and other consumer and trade publications.

Carnicon's corporate public relations department is here to help you develop those opportunities and make sure the news media knows about them. . . .

But news is what's happening to the resort and you *when it happens.* We need to take advantage of opportunities to send out information, and—perhaps more importantly—to get photography, when the news is *immediate!* Once the people are gone and the events are over, we can't make that particular news ever happen again.

This manual explores:

- What public relations *really* is;
- How it can directly benefit your sales efforts;
- What your property's sales staff can do to get an edge on the competition;
- How you can work with the Carnicon Corporate Public Relations Department for maximum benefit.

II. DEFINING PUBLIC RELATIONS

In a pure sense public relations encompasses the many forms of communication that a company uses to inform its *publics* or markets, including messages via mass media and other more direct, personal, or informal communications.

As it is more commonly defined, public relations is what companies do to draw positive attention to themselves, mostly in partnership with news media and/or via promotions.

The activities that the Carnicon Corporate Public Relations Department performs for you are:

- Distributing News Announcements to international media,
- Bringing writers and editors to your property from

your key international target markets so they can write about you,

- Promoting events and cooperative promotional activities,
- Assisting with other forms of communications (i.e., crisis communications).

III. HOW PUBLIC RELATIONS WORKS FOR YOUR SALES EFFORT

By getting your name and picture or our clients' names and pictures in the travel and meeting trade news media, public relations constantly reinforces through a *third party endorsement* that you are a top property!

In addition, public relations can help your clients sell your hotel:

- Associations often need help communicating with their members.
- Travel agents may need to promote special packages.
- Meeting planners will remember your sales visit while forgetting many others.
- You can help clients get on the radio, in their local newspapers, or in their trade publication.

IV. WHAT DOES THE NEWS MEDIA WANT?

The job of the writer and editor is to tell the truth to the best of their ability. While advertising is paid for and advertisers can say whatever they want, the public relations person must convince the editor that he/she is telling a story that the editor—and audience—wants to hear.

The sales department is close to the news of the industry. In the course of one day, they probably come across 10 things that would be of interest to the news. *Many of them you don't want published.* By working closely with your sales manager, you can help to identify appropriate news items that will help put your property in the media spotlight! These newsworthy items may include:

- Trends in bookings. Did 45 Australian travel agencies suddenly request information about your hotel? Is a meeting, that has been held for 10 years in Botswana, suddenly moving to your area?
- Records. Did your hotel sell out for 30 consecutive days?

- Names. Is the owner of the largest incentive company in North America coming to your hotel this weekend?
- Unusual activities. Did a group construct a replica wooden ship on the beach for a "Columbus' Discovery" theme party?

Be aware of these and other opportunities. You are the best source of information for our public relations effort and these opportunities can make your hotel more famous than it already is!

V. PHOTOGRAPHY, PHOTOGRAPHY AND MORE PHOTOGRAPHY!
The meeting and travel trade publics are constantly in need of good photography of agents and their suppliers.
Some tried and true subjects for photography include:

- *On-Site*—Pictures of planners at your hotel during a fam, if taken properly, will usually get published.
- *Celebrating Together*—Do you have VIPs on the property during the General Manager's birthday party? Has someone won a trip to your hotel? Is a tennis or golf clinic being held especially for travel agents?
- *On the Road*—Have you brought your favorite New York City client a special souvenir in the middle of winter? Are you personally delivering the *largest monthly commission check in your hotel's history?*

VI. INTERVIEW OPPORTUNITIES
The meeting trade publications are always looking for information that can come only from the sales and convention services departments.

Some of the magazines will run pictures like the ones described above, however, they are also interested in "how to do it," "innovative ideas," and "case studies."

These offer us an opportunity for major exposure, and must be planned well in advance between you and the Carnicon Corporate Public Relations Department.

Remember "Columbus' Discovery"? That is just what the magazines are looking for! If we know about it in advance, we can get a writer to cover the meeting creating positive exposure for your hotel and client.

- Has your hotel solved a particular meeting problem?
- Has your banqueting department resolved a particularly difficult request for a client that resulted in a win-win situation?

- Have you been able to offer a client something he has never received anywhere else before?

Let's discuss it as soon as possible so that you and your client can get the proper recognition!

VII. PROMOTIONS

Has your sales department offered a free trip to your property as part of a sales promotion? By getting a photograph of the prize winner enjoying your hotel, we can garner additional publicity from the promotion by sending a short story and photo to the winner's hometown newspaper. Friends and neighbors will all want to know about the winner's exciting vacation at your property. Remember, word-of-mouth is one of the world's strongest sales tools.

Are you planning a special event involving corporate sponsors? Make sure to invite the media as your guest to participate—and write about—your event.

Do you have an upcoming event that involves international guests or sponsors? Contact Carnicon's corporate public relations department as soon as you start planning the event and we'll assist you in generating international exposure for your event. If there is enough lead time, we may even be able to attract additional guests to the hotel for the event.

THE TEN COMMANDMENTS OF PR

1. Keep in mind who your audience is—always target your message, whether written or spoken, to the people who will ultimately read or listen to it.
2. Be aware of deadlines! Always send your news releases with enough advance notice and *never* call an editor when they are on deadline.
3. Do not exaggerate or speculate. It is always better for an editor to be pleasantly surprised that something is bigger, better, or more impressive than you described, than to be disappointed because of inflated expectations.
4. Call before writing. Get to know the editors/writers in your area personally.
5. Follow up. After a writer visits your property, send a personal note thanking them for visiting and inviting

them to return in the future. You'll be surprised how many of them continue writing about your property for years after their visit.

6. Public relations opportunities are timely. Respond quickly with correct information and appropriate photos to get the best exposure.

7. Listen, watch, and read. Know what the media is currently covering, so that you don't send inappropriate information or contact the wrong journalist. You may see an opportunity for your property to be included in the news by offering an appropriate spokesperson on a local issue, creating a fundraiser to answer a special need in the community, etc.

8. Be a resource. Stay in contact with key writers/editors and know what their needs are so that you can supply them with interesting information they want to write about.

9. Be friendly, professional, and courteous. Journalists are not always the easiest people to deal with because they are under tremendous pressure. They like to work with PR professionals who help them fill their pages with interesting news *and* meet their deadlines.

10. Enjoy yourself! Public relations puts you in touch with your guests, the community, your management and staff, and the media. You are the catalyst for bringing all of these people together to celebrate what makes your property special. So be careful— your enthusiasm will be contagious![1]

Exhibit 11-1. Public Relations Manual. Excerpts from the Public Relations Manual for Sales Managers prepared by Carnival Hotels & Casinos (CHC).*

NOTE

1. Carnival Hotels & Casinos, Public Relations Manual for Sales Managers.

* Reprinted courtesy of Carnival Hotels & Casinos.

American Hotel & Motel Association Member State Associations

Alabama Hotel & Motel Association
660 Adams Avenue, Ste. 254
Montgomery, AL 36014
(205)263-3407
(205)263-3426 (fax)

Alaska Hotel-Motel Association
P.O. Box 104900,
  340 E. 4th Ave.
Anchorage, AK 99510
(907)272-1229
(907)265-5146 (fax)

Arizona Hotel & Motel Association
2201 E. Camelback Road,
  Ste. 125B
Phoenix, AZ 85016
(602)553-8802
(602)553-8154 (fax)

Arkansas Hospitality Association
P.O. Box 3866/603 Pulaski St.
Little Rock, AR 72203/72201
(501)376-2323
(501)376-6517(fax)

California Hotel & Motel Association
P.O. Box 160405,
  414 29th Street
Sacramento, CA 95816
(916)444-5780, 5781
(916)444-5848 (fax)

Colorado Hotel & Lodging Association
999 18th Street, Ste. 1240
Denver, CO 80202
(303)297-8335
(303)297-8104 (fax)

Connecticut Lodging & Attractions Assn.
15 Farm Springs Road
Farmington, CT 06032
(203)678-7299
(203)677-8770 (fax)

Delaware Hotel-Motel Association
c/o Richard Encarnacao
Christiana Hilton Inn
100 Continental Drive
Wilmington, DE 19713
(302)454-1500
(302)454-0233 (fax)

Hotel Association of Washington DC
1201 New York Avenue, NW, Suite 601
Washington, DC 20005
(202)289-3141
(202)289-3199 (fax)

Florida Hotel & Motel Association
200 West College Avenue
Tallahassee, FL 32301
(800)476-3462
(904)224-2888
(904)222-3462 (fax)

Georgia Hospitality & Travel Association
600 W. Peachtree St., N.W., Ste. 1500
Atlanta, GA 30308
(404)873-4482
(404)874-5742 (fax)

Hawaii Hotel Association
2270 Kalakaua Avenue, #1103
Honolulu, HI 96815
(808)923-0407
(808)924-3843 (fax)

Idaho Hospitality & Travel Association
P.O. Box 7587, 4930 Umatilla
Boise, ID 83707
(208)362-2637
(208)362-0855 (fax)

Hotel-Motel Association of Illinois
27 East Monroe Street, Ste. 700
Chicago, IL 60603
(312)346-3135
(312)346-6036 (fax)

Hotel-Motel Association of Illinois
5A Lawrence Square
Springfield, IL 62704
(217)522-1231
(217)522-2419 (fax)

Indiana Hotel & Motel Association
8041 Knue Road, #109
Indianapolis, IN 46250
(317)577-4800
(317)577-4801 (fax)

Iowa Lodging Association
9001 Hickman Road, Ste. 2B
Des Moines, IA 50322-5306
(515)278-8700
(515)278-0245 (fax)

Kansas Lodging Association
700 S.W. Jackson St., Ste. 702
Topeka, KS 66603-3740
(913)233-9344
(913)357-6629 (fax)

Kentucky Hotel & Motel Association
P.O. Box 1183
Frankfort, KY 40602
(502)875-1115
(502)875-7536 (fax)

Louisiana Hotel-Motel Association

150 Baronne Street, Suite 513
New Orleans, LA 70112
(504)525-9326
(504)525-9327 (fax)

Maine Innkeepers Association

305 Commercial Street
Portland, ME 04101-4641
(207)773-7670
(207)773-7668 (fax)

Maryland Hotel & Motel Association

584 Bellerive Drive, Suite 3D
Annapolis, MD 21401
(410)974-4472
(410)757-3809 (fax)

Massachusetts Lodging Association

7 Liberty Square, 2nd Floor
Boston, MA 02109
(617)720-1776
(617)720-1305 (fax)

Michigan Hotel, Motel, & Resort Association

6105 W. St. Joseph, Ste. 204
Lansing, MI 48917
(517)323-1818
(517)323-1994 (fax)

Minnesota Hotel & Lodging Association

871 Jefferson Avenue
St. Paul, MN 55102
(612)222-7401, 222-4906
(612)222-7347 (fax)

Mississippi Hotel & Motel Association

5135 Galaxie Drive, Ste. 203-B
Jackson, MS 39206
(601)981-1160
(601)981-1217 (fax)

Missouri Hotel & Motel Association

101 East High Street
Jefferson City, MO 65101
(314)636-2107
(314)635-6258 (fax)

Montana Innkeepers Association

P.O. Box 1272, 15 W. 6th Ave.,
Ste. 507
Helena, MT 59624
(406)449-8408
(406)442-8018 (fax)

Nebraska Lodging Association

1111 Lincoln Mall, Ste. 308
Lincoln, NE 68508
(402)476-1528
(402)476-1259 (fax)

Nevada Hotel & Motel Association

4820 Alpine Place, Ste. B202
Las Vegas, NV 89107
(702)878-9272
(702)878-5009 (fax)

New Hampshire Lodging & Restaurant Association

4 Park Street, Ste. 403
(P.O. Box 1175, 03302-1175)
Concord, NH 03301
(603)228-9585
(603)226-1829 (fax)

New Jersey Hotel-Motel Association
Lexington Square Commons
2137 Route #33, Ste. 1
Trenton, NJ 08690
(609)586-9000
(609)586-9010 (fax)

New Mexico Hotel-Motel Association
1478 South St. Francis Dr.
P.O. Box 2534
Santa Fe, NM 87504
(505)983-4554
(505)982-9359 (fax)

Hotel Association of New York City, Inc.
437 Madison Avenue
New York, NY 10022
(212)754-6700
(212)754-0243 (fax)

New York State Hospitality & Tourism Association
11 North Pearl Street,
  11th Floor
Albany, NY 12207
(518)465-2300
(518)465-4025 (fax)

North Carolina Hotel & Motel Association
4101 Lake Boone Trail, Ste. 201
Raleigh, NC 27607
(919)787-5181
(919)787-4916 (fax)

North Dakota Hospitality Association
P.O. Box 428
  (919 S. 7th Ave. 58504)
Bismarck, ND 58502
(701)223-3313
(701)223-0215 (fax)

Ohio Hotel & Motel Association
692 North High Street, St. 212
Columbus, OH 43215
(614)461-6462
(614)224-4714 (fax)

Oklahoma Hotel & Motel Association
3800 N. Portland
Oklahoma City, OK 73112
(405)942-8181
(800)375-8181
(405)942-0541 (fax)

Oregon Lodging Association
12724 SE Stark Street
Portland, OR 97233
(503)255-5135
(503)255-4927 (fax)

Pennsylvania Travel Council
902 North Second Street
Harrisburg, PA 17102
(717)232-8880
(717)232-8948 (fax)

Rhode Island Hospitality Association
P.O. Box 6208
(1206 Jefferson Blvd.
Warwick, RI 02886)
Providence, RI 02940
(401)732-4881
(401)732-4883 (fax)

The Hospitality Association of South Carolina
1338 Main Street, Ste. 505
Columbia, SC 29201-3219
(803)765-9000
(803)252-7136 (fax)

South Dakota Innkeepers Association
809 West Avenue North
Sioux Falls, SD 57104
(605)331-4194
(605)331-4194 (fax)

Tennessee Hotel & Motel Association
644 West Iris Drive
Nashville, TN 37204
(615)385-9970
(615)385-9957 (fax)

Texas Hotel & Motel Association
900 Congress Avenue, Ste. 310
Austin, TX 78701
(512)474-2996
(512)480-0773 (fax)

Utah Hotel-Motel Association
9 Exchange Place, Ste. 812
Salt Lake City, UT 84111
(801)359-0104
(801)359-0105 (fax)

Vermont Lodging & Restaurant Association
Route 100 North, RI, #1522
Waterbury, VT 05676
(802)244-1344
(802)244-1342 (fax)

Virginia Hospitality & Travel Industry Association
2101 Libbie Avenue
Richmond, VA 23230-2621
(804)288-3065
(804)285-3093 (fax)

Washington State Hotel & Motel Association
3605 132nd Avenue SE, Ste. 320
Bellevue, WA 98006
(206)957-4585
(206)957-4587 (fax)

West Virginia Hospitality & Travel Association
2720 Penn Avenue
Charleston, WV 25302
P.O. Box 239
Charleston, WV 25328
(304)342-6511
(304)345-1538 (fax)

Wisconsin Innkeepers Association
509 W. Wisconsin Avenue, Ste. 729
Milwaukee, WI 53203
(414)271-2851
(414)271-3050 (fax)

Wyoming Lodging & Restaurant Association
1723 Thomes Ste. B,
(P.O. Box 1003, 82003)
Cheyenne, WY 82001
(307)634-8816
(307)632-0249 (fax)

B

State Administrative Officials: Tourism 1993–1994: The Council of State Governments

---

Alabama
Department of Tourism & Travel
   401 Adams Ave., Ste. 126
   Montgomery, AL 36104
   (205)242-4169

Alaska
Division of Tourism
Department of Commerce & Economic Development
   P.O. Box 110801
   Juneau, AK 99811
   (907)465-2010

Arizona
Office of Tourism
   1100 W. Washington
   Phoenix, AZ 85007
   (602)542-8687

Arkansas
Tourism Division
Department of Parks & Tourism
   One Capitol Mall
   Little Rock, AR 72201
   (501)682-1088

California
Office of Tourism
   801 K St., Ste. 1600
   Sacramento, CA 95814
   (916)322-2881

Colorado
Tourism Board
Department of Local Affairs
   1625 Broadway, Rm. 1700
   Denver, CO 80202
   (303)592-5410

Connecticut
Tourism Division
Department of Economic
Development
  865 Brook St.
  Rocky Hill, CT 06067
  (203)258-4286

Delaware
Tourism Office
Development Office
  P.O. Box 1401
  Dover, DE 19901
  (302)736-4271

Florida
Division of Tourism
Department of Commerce
  107 W. Gaines St., #324-A
  Tallahassee, FL 32399
  (904)488-5607

Georgia
Tourist Division
Industry, Trade & Tourism
  285 Peachtree Ctr. Ave.,
  #1000
  Atlanta, GA 30303
  (404)656-3556

Hawaii
Department of Business,
Economic Development &
Tourism
  220 S. King St., #1100
  Honolulu, HI 96813
  (808)586-2359

Idaho
Tourism Development
Department of Commerce
  700 W. State St.
  Boise, ID 83720
  (208)334-2470

Illinois
Department of Commerce &
Community Affairs
  620 E. Adams St., 3rd Fl.
  Springfield, IL 62701
  (217)782-3233

Indiana
Tourism Development
Department of Commerce
  1 N. Capitol
  Indianapolis, IN 46204
  (317)232-8870

Iowa
Division of Tourism & Visitors
Department of Economic
Development
  200 E. Grand
  Des Moines, IA 50309
  (515)242-4705

Kansas
Division of Travel & Tourism
Department of Commerce
& Housing
  700 S.W. Harrison, Ste. 1300
  Topeka, KS 66603
  (913)296-7091

Kentucky
Tourism Cabinet
  Capital Plaza Tower
  Frankfort, KY 40601
  (502)564-4270

Louisiana
Office of Tourism
Department of Culture,
Recreation & Tourism
  P.O. Box 94291
  Baton Rouge, LA 70804
  (504)342-8125

Maine
Division of Tourism
Department of Economic &
Community Development
State House Station #59
Augusta, ME 04333
(207)287-5711

Maryland
Office of Tourism & Promotion
Office of Economic &
Employment Development
217 E. Redwood St.
Baltimore, MD 21202
(410)333-6611

Massachusetts
Travel & Tourism, Executive
Office of Economic Affairs
100 Cambridge St., 13th Fl.
Boston, MA 02202
(617)727-3201

Michigan
Travel Bureau
Department of Commerce
333 S. Capitol Ave.
Lansing, MI 48909
(517)335-1879

Minnesota
Office of Tourism
100 Metro Sq. Bldg.
121 7th Pl., E.
St. Paul, MN 55101
(612)296-2755

Mississippi
Division of Tourism
Department of Economic &
Community Development
P.O. Box 849
Jackson, MS 39205
(601)359-3449

Missouri
Division of Tourism
Department of Economic
Development
P.O. Box 1055
Jefferson City, MO 65102
(314)751-4133

Montana
Promotion Bureau
Department of Commerce
1424 Ninth Ave.
Helena, MT 59620
(406)444-2654

Nebraska
Division of Travel & Tourism
Department of Economic
Development
P.O. Box 94666
Lincoln, NE 68509
(402)471-3794

Nevada
Commission on Tourism
5151 S. Carson St.
Carson City, NV 89710
(702)687-4322

New Hampshire
Vacation Travel Promotion
Office
Department of Resources &
Economic Development
172 Pembroke Rd.
Concord, NH 03301
(603)271-2665

New Jersey
Division of Travel & Tourism
Department of Commerce &
Economic Development
20 W. State St., CN826
Trenton, NJ 08625
(609)292-2470

New Mexico
Tourism Division
 1100 St. Francis Dr.
 Santa Fe, NM 87503
 (505)827-0291

New York
Department of Commerce
 1 Commerce Plz.
 Albany, NY 12245
 (518)474-4100

North Carolina
Travel Development Division
Department of Commerce
 430 N. Salisbury St.
 Raleigh, NC 27603
 (919)733-4171

North Dakota
Department of Parks &
Recreation
 Liberty Memorial Bldg.
 604 E. Boulevard Ave.
 Bismarck, ND 58505
 (701)224-2525

Ohio
Office of Travel & Tourism
Department of Development
 30 E. Broad St., 25th Fl.
 Columbus, OH 43266
 (614)466-8844

Oklahoma
Department of Tourism &
Recreation
 500 Will Rogers Bldg.
 Oklahoma City, OK 73105
 (405)521-2413

Oregon
Tourism Division
Department of Economic
Development
 775 Summer St.
 Salem, OR 97310
 (503)373-1230

Pennsylvania
Department of Commerce
 433 Forum Bldg.
 Harrisburg, PA 17120
 (717)783-3840

Rhode Island
Department of Economic
Development
 7 Jackson Walkway
 Providence, RI 02903
 (401)277-2601

South Carolina
Division of Tourism
Department of Parks,
Recreation & Tourism
 1205 Pendleton St.
 Columbia, SC 29201
 (803)734-0135

South Dakota
Department of Tourism
 Capitol Lake Plz.
 Pierre, SD 57501
 (605)773-3301

Tennessee
Department of Tourist
Development
 320 Sixth Ave., N.
 Nashville, TN 37243
 (615)741-9001

Texas
Department of Commerce
P.O. Box 12728
Austin, TX 78711
(512)472-5059

Utah
Division of Travel
Development
Department of Community &
Economic Development
Council Hall
Capitol Hill
Salt Lake City, UT 84114
(801)538-1030

Vermont
Travel Division
Agency of Development &
Community Affairs
134 State St.
Montpelier, VT 05602
(802)828-3236

Virginia
Division of Tourism
Department of Economic
Development
1021 E. Cary St.
Richmond, VA 23219
(804)786-2051

Washington
Tourism Development
Department of Trade &
Economic Development
P.O. Box 42500
Olympia, WA 98504
(206)753-5601

West Virginia
Division of Tourism & Parks
Bldg. 6, Rm. 451
1900 Kanawha Blvd., E.
Charleston, WV 25305
(304)558-2764

Wisconsin
Division of Tourism
Development
Department of Development
P.O. Box 7970
Madison, WI 53707
(608)266-2147

Wyoming
Tourism Division
Department of Commerce
I-25 at College Dr.
Cheyenne, WY 82002
(307)777-7777

Washington, D.C.
Washington Convention Ctr.
900 Ninth St., N.W.
Washington, DC 20004
(202)789-1600

Washington, D.C.
D.C. Visitors & Convention
Association
1212 New York Ave., N.W.,
Ste. 600
Washington, DC 20005
(202)789-7000

Washington, D.C.
Office of Tourism &
Promotions
1212 New York Ave., N.W.,
Ste. 200
Washington, DC 20005
(202)727-4511

Washington, D.C.
Committee to Promote
Washington
  1212 New York Ave., N.W.,
    #200
  Washington, DC 20005
  (202)724-4091

American Samoa
Office of Tourism
  Pago Pago, AS 96799
  (684)633-1092

Guam
Visitors Bureau
  P.O. Box 3520
  Agana, GU 96910
  (671)646-5278

Commonwealth of Northern
Mariana Islands
Visitors Bureau
Office of the Governor
  Saipan, MP 96950
  (670)234-8325

Puerto Rico
Tourism Co.
  P.O. Box 4435
  San Juan, PR 00903
  (809)721-2400

U.S. Virgin Islands
Department of Economic
Development & Agriculture
  P.O. Box 6400
  St. Thomas, VI 00802
  (809)774-8784

APPENDIX

C

State Administrative Officials: Economic Development 1993–1994: The Council of State Governments

Alabama
Department of Economic &
Community Affairs
P.O. Box 5690
Montgomery, AL 36103
(205)242-5100

Alaska
Economic Development
Department of Commerce &
Economic Development
P.O. Box 110804
Juneau, AK 99811
(907)465-2017

Arizona
Department of Commerce
3800 N. Central Ave.
Phoenix, AZ 85012
(602)280-1306

Arkansas
Industrial Development
Commission
1 Capitol Mall, Rm. 4C-300
Little Rock, AR 72201
(501)682-2052

California
Trade & Commerce Agency
801 K St., Ste. 1700
Sacramento, CA 95814
(916)322-3962

Colorado
Office of Business
Development
Office of Governor
1625 Broadway, Ste. 1710
Denver, CO 80202
(303)892-3840

Connecticut
Department of Economic
Development
865 Brook St.
Rocky Hill, CT 06067
(203)258-4201

Delaware
Development Office
P.O. Box 1401
Dover, DE 19903
(302)739-4271

Florida
Division of Economic
Development
Department of Commerce
501B Collins Bldg.
Tallahassee, FL 32399
(904)488-6300

Georgia
Department of Industry, Trade
& Tourism
285 Peachtree Center Ave., N.E.,
Ste. 1000
Atlanta, GA 30303
(404)656-3556

Hawaii
Department of Business,
Economic Development &
Tourism
220 S. King St., #1100
Honolulu, HI 96813
(808)586-2355

Idaho
Division of Economic
Development
Department of Commerce
700 W. State St.
Boise, ID 83720
(208)334-2470

Illinois
Department of Commerce &
Community Affairs
620 E. Adams St., 3rd Fl.
Springfield, IL 62701
(217)782-3233

Indiana
Business Development &
Marketing Group
Department of Commerce
1 N. Capitol, Ste. 700
Indianapolis, IN 46204
(317)232-0159

Iowa
Department of Economic
Development
200 E. Grand
Des Moines, IA 50309
(515)242-4814

Kansas
Department of Commerce
& Housing
700 S.W. Harrison, Ste. 1300
Topeka, KS 66603
(913)296-3480

Kansas
Division of Existing Industry
Department of Commerce
& Housing
700 S.W. Harrison, Ste. 1300
Topeka, KS 66603
(913)296-5298

Kansas
Division of Industrial
Development
Department of Commerce
& Housing
700 S.W. Harrison, Ste. 1300
Topeka, KS 66603
(913)296-2652

Kansas
Kansas, Inc.
  632-S.W. Van Buren St.,
  Ste. 100
  Topeka, KS 66603
  (913)296-1460

Kentucky
Cabinet for Economic
Development
  Capital Plaza Tower, 23rd Fl.
  500 Mero St.
  Frankfort, KY 40601
  (502)564-7670

Louisiana
Department of Economic
Development
  P.O. Box 94185
  Baton Rouge, LA 70804
  (504)342-5388

Maine
Department of Economic &
Community Development
  State House Station #59
  Augusta, ME 04333
  (207)287-2656

Maryland
Department of Economic &
Employment Development
  217 E. Redwood St.
  Baltimore, MD 21202
  (410)333-6901

Massachusetts
Executive Office of Economic
Affairs
  1 Ashburton Pl., Rm. 2101
  Boston, MA 02108
  (617)727-8380

Michigan
Manufacturing Development
Department of Commerce
  P.O. Box 30225
  Lansing, MI 48909
  (517)373-0347

Minnesota
Economic Development
Division
Department of Business
Development
  500 Metro Sq.
  121 9th Pl., E.
  St. Paul, MN 55101
  (612)296-5005

Mississippi
Department of Economic &
Community Development
  P.O. Box 849
  Jackson, MS 39205
  (601)359-3449

Missouri
Department of Economic
Development
  301 W. High St.
  P.O. Box 1157
  Jefferson City, MO 65102
  (314)751-3946

Montana
Business Development
Division
Department of Commerce
  1424 Ninth Ave.
  Helena, MT 59620
  (406)444-3923

Nebraska
Department of Economic
Development
  301 Centennial Mall S.
  P.O. Box 94666
  Lincoln, NE 68509
  (402)471-3111

Nevada
Commission on Economic
Development
  5151 S. Carson St.
  Carson City, NV 89710
  (702)687-4325

New Hampshire
Office of Business &
Industrial Development
Division of Economic
Development
  P.O. Box 856
  Concord, NH 03301
  (603)271-2591

New Jersey
Division of Economic
Development
Department of Commerce &
Economic Development
  20 W. State St., CN823
  Trenton, NJ 08625
  (609)292-7757

New Mexico
Department of Economic
Development
  1100 St. Francis Dr.
  Santa Fe, NM 87503
  (505)827-0380

New York
Department of Commerce
  1 Commerce Plz.
  Albany, NY 12245
  (518)474-4100

North Carolina
Business/Industry Development
Department of Commerce
  430 N. Salisbury St.
  Raleigh, NC 27603
  (919)733-4151

North Dakota
Economic Development
& Finance
  1833 E. Bismarck Expy.
  Bismarck, ND 58504
  (701)221-5300

Ohio
Department of Development
  77 S. High St., 29th Fl.
  Columbus, OH 43266
  (614)466-3379

Oklahoma
Department of Commerce
  6601 Broadway Ext.
  Oklahoma City, OK 73116
  (405)843-9770

Oregon
Business Development
Department of Economic
Development
  595 Cottage St., N.E.
  Salem, OR 97310
  (503)373-1225

Pennsylvania
Department of Commerce
  433 Forum Bldg.
  Harrisburg, PA 17120
  (717)783-3840

Rhode Island
Department of Economic
Development
  7 Jackson Walkway
  Providence, RI 02903
  (401)277-2601

South Carolina
Department of Commerce
P.O. Box 927
Columbia, SC 29202
(803)737-0400

South Dakota
Governor's Office of Economic
Development
Capitol Lake Plz.
Pierre, SD 57501
(605)773-5032

Tennessee
Department of Economic &
Community Development
320 Sixth Ave., N., 8th Fl.
Nashville, TN 37243
(615)741-1888

Texas
Department of Commerce
P.O. Box 12728
Austin, TX 78711
(512)472-5059

Utah
Division of Business &
Economic Development
Department of Community &
Economic Development
324 S. State St., Ste. 200
Salt Lake City, UT 84111
(801)538-8810

Vermont
Department of Economic
Development
109 State St.
Montpelier, VT 05602
(802)828-3221

Virginia
Commerce & Trade
202 N. Ninth St., Rm. 723
Richmond, VA 23219
(804)786-7831

Virginia
Department of Economic
Development
1021 E. Cary St.
Richmond, VA 23219
(804)371-8100

Washington
Department of Trade &
Economic Development
101 General Administration
  Bldg.
P.O. Box 42500
Olympia, WA 98504
(206)753-7426

West Virginia
Development Office
Bldg. 6, Rm. 504
1900 Kanawha Blvd., E.
Charleston, WV 25305
(304)558-2234

Wisconsin
Bureau of Business
Expansion & Recruitment
Department of Development
P.O. Box 7970
Madison, WI 53707
(608)266-1018

Wyoming
Division of Economic &
Community Development
Department of Commerce
2301 Central Ave. 4 N
Cheyenne, WY 82002
(307)777-6435

Washington, DC
Economic Development Office
Office of the Mayor
441 4th St., N.W., 11th Fl.
Washington, DC 20001
(202)727-6365

American Samoa
Office of Economic
Development Planning
Utulei
Pago Pago, AS 96799
(684)633-5155

Guam
Economic Development
Authority
590 S. Marine Dr., Ste. 911
Tamuning, GU 96911
(671)646-4141

Commonwealth of Northern
Mariana Islands
Commonwealth Development
Authority
P.O. Box 2149
Saipan, MP 96950
(670)234-7145

Commonwealth of Northern
Mariana Islands
Department of Commerce
& Labor
Office of the Governor
Saipan, MP 96950
(670)322-4361

Puerto Rico
Industrial Development Co.
P.O. Box 362350
San Juan, PR 00936
(809)764-3175

U.S. Virgin Islands
Department of Economic
Development & Agriculture
P.O. Box 6400
St. Thomas, VI 00804
(809)774-8784

Copyright 1993. The Council of State Governments. Reprinted with permission from *State Administrative Officials Classified by Function.*

D

State Restaurant Associations*

Alabama Restaurant and Foodservice Association
2100 Data Drive, Suite 207
Birmingham, AL 35244
(205)988-9880
(205)988-5055 (fax)

Alaska Cabaret, Hotel and Restaurant Association
341 East 56th Avenue
Anchorage, AK 99518
(907)563-8133
(907)563-8640 (fax)

Arizona Restaurant Association
2701 North 16th Street,
 Suite 221
Phoenix, AZ 85006
(602)234-0701
(602)266-6043 (fax)

Arkansas Hospitality Association
603 Pulaski Street
P.O. Box 1556
Little Rock, AR 72203
(501)376-2323
(501)376-6517 (fax)

California Restaurant Association
3435 Wilshire Boulevard,
 Suite 2606
Los Angeles, CA 90010
(213)384-1200
(213)384-1623 (fax)

---

* Reprinted by permission. List provided by National Restaurant Association State Relations & Grassroots Programs:
 1200 Seventeenth Street N.W.
 Washington, DC 20036
 202-331-5900, 800-424-5156
 202-331-2429 (fax)

Government Affairs Office California Restaurant Association
980 9th Street, Suite 1480
Sacramento, CA 95814
(916)447-5793
(916)447-6182 (fax)

Colorado Restaurant Association
899 Logan Street, Suite 300
Denver, CO 80203
(303)830-2972
(303)830-2973 (fax)

Connecticut Restaurant Association
731 Hebron Avenue
Glastonbury, CT 06033
(203)633-5484
(203)657-8241 (fax)

Delaware Restaurant Association
P.O. Box 7838
Newark, DE 19714-7838
(302)366-8565
(302)738-8865 (fax)

Restaurant Association of Metropolitan Washington, Inc.
7926 Jones Branch Drive, Suite 530
McLean, VA 22102-3303
(703)356-1315
(703)893-4926 (fax)

Florida Restaurant Association
2441 Hollywood Boulevard
Hollywood, FL 33020-6605
(305)921-6300
(305)925-6381 (fax)

Georgia Hospitality and Travel Association
600 West Peachtree Street, Suite 1500
Atlanta, GA 30308
(404)873-4482
(404)874-5742 (fax)

Hawaii Restaurant Association
1188 Bishop Street, Suite 1507
Honolulu, HI 96813
(808)536-9105
(808)536-9106 (fax)

Idaho Hospitality & Travel Association, Inc.
P.O. Box 7587
Boise, ID 83707
(208)362-2637
(208)362-0855 (fax)

Illinois Restaurant Association
350 West Ontario
Chicago, IL 60610
(312)787-4000
(312)787-4792 (fax)

Restaurant and Hospitality Association of Indiana
2120 North Meridian Street
Indianapolis, IN 46202
(317)924-5106
(317)921-3865 (fax)

Iowa Restaurant and Beverage Association
606 Merle Hay Tower
Des Moines, IA 50310
(515)276-1454
(515)276-3660 (fax)

Kansas Restaurant and Hospitality Association
359 South Hydraulic
Wichita, KS 67211
(316)267-8383
(316)267-8400 (fax)

Kentucky Restaurant Association
422 Executive Park
Louisville, KY 40207
(502)896-0464
(502)896-0465 (fax)

Louisiana Restaurant Association
2800 Veterans Boulevard,
  Suite 160
Metairie, LA 70002
(504)831-7788
(504)837-4967 (fax)

Maine Restaurant Association
Five Wade Street, P.O. Box 5060
Augusta, ME 04330-0552
(207)623-2178
(207)623-8377 (fax)

Restaurant Association of Maryland, Inc.
7113 Ambassador Road
Baltimore, MD 21244
(410)298-0011
(410)298-0299 (fax)

Massachusetts Restaurant Association
95-A Turnpike Road
Westborough, MA 01581-9775
(508)366-4144
(508)366-4614 (fax)

Massachusetts Restaurant Association
141 Tremont Street, 6th Floor
Boston, MA 02111
(617)426-1081
(617)426-8564 (fax)

Michigan Restaurant Association
225 West Washtenaw
Lansing, MI 48933
(517)482-5244
(517)482-7663 (fax)

Minnesota Restaurant Association
871 Jefferson Avenue
St. Paul, MN 55102
(612)222-7401
(612)222-7347

Mississippi Restaurant Association
P.O. Box 16395
Jackson, MS 39236
(601)982-4281
(601)982-0062 (fax)

Missouri Restaurant Association
P.O. Box 10277
Kansas City, MO 64171
(816)753-5222
(816)753-6993 (fax)

Montana Restaurant Association
Box 7998
Missoula, MT 59807
(406)721-2895, (406)543-8265
(406)543-0893 (fax)

Nebraska Restaurant Association
5625 "O" St. Building, Suite 7
Lincoln, NE 68510
(402)483-2630
(402)483-2746 (fax)

Nevada Restaurant Association
4820 Alpine Place, Suite B202
Las Vegas, NV 89107
(702)878-2313
(702)878-5009 (fax)

New Hampshire Lodging and Restaurant Association
P.O. Box 1175, 4 Park Street,
  Suite 413
Concord, NH 03301
(603)228-9585
(603)226-1829 (fax)

New Jersey Restaurant Association
One Executive Drive, Suite 100
Somerset, NJ 08873
(908)302-1800
(908)302-1804 (fax)

New Mexico Restaurant Association
7800 Marble, NE Suite 4
Albuquerque, NM 87110
(505)268-2474
(505)268-5848

New York State Restaurant Association
505 Eighth Avenue, 7th Floor
New York, NY 10018
(212)714-1330
(212)643-2962 (fax)

New York State Restaurant Association
455 New Karner Road
Albany, NY 12205
(518)452-4222
(518)452-4497 (fax)

North Carolina Restaurant Association
P.O. Box 6528
Raleigh, NC 27628
(919)782-5022
(919)782-7251 (fax)

North Dakota State Hospitality Association
P.O. Box 428
Bismarck, ND 58502
(701)223-3313
(701)223-0215 (fax)

Ohio Restaurant Association
1335 Dublin Road
Suite 208D
Columbus, OH 43215
(614)488-3848
(614)488-4053 (fax)

Oklahoma Restaurant Association
3800 North Portland
Oklahoma City, OK 73112
(405)942-8181
(405)942-0541 (fax)

Oregon Restaurant Association
8565 SW Salish Lane,
Suite #120
Wilsonville, OR 97070
(503)682-4422
(503)682-4455 (fax)

Pennsylvania Restaurant Association
100 State Street
Harrisburg, PA 17101-1024
(717)232-4433
(717)236-1202 (fax)

Rhode Island Hospitality Association
Box 6208
Providence, RI 02940
(401)732-4881
(401)732-4883 (fax)

South Carolina Restaurant Association
Barringer Building, Suite 505
1338 Main Street
Columbia, SC 29201
(803)765-9000
(803)252-7136 (fax)

South Dakota Restaurant Association
P.O. Box 1173
Pierre, SD 57501
(605)224-0127
(605)224-9005 (fax)

Tennessee Restaurant Association
P.O. Box 681207
Franklin, TN 37068-1207
(615)790-2703
(615)790-2768 (fax)

Texas Restaurant Association
P.O. Box 1429
Austin, TX 78767
(512)472-3666
(512)472-2777 (fax)

Utah Restaurant Association
141 Haven Avenue, Suite 2
Salt Lake City, UT 84115
(801)487-4821
(801)486-4367 (fax)

Vermont Lodging and Restaurant Association
Route 100 North, R1, #1522
Waterbury, VT 05676
(802)244-1344
(802)244-1342 (fax)

Virginia Hospitality & Travel Industry Association/Restaurant Division
2101 Libbic Avenue
Richmond, VA 23230
(804)288-3065
(804)285-3093 (fax)

Restaurant Association of the State of Washington, Inc.
2405 Evergreen Park Drive, SW, Suite A2
Olympia, WA 98502
(206)956-7279
(206)357-9232 (fax)

West Virginia Hospitality and Travel Association
P.O. Box 2391
Charleston, WV 25328
(304)342-6511
(304)345-1538 (fax)

Wisconsin Restaurant Association
31 South Henry Street, Suite 300
Madison, WI 53703-3110
(608)251-3663
(608)251-3666 (fax)

Wyoming Lodging & Restaurant Association
P.O. Box 1003
Cheyenne, WY 82003-1003
(307)634-8816
(307)632-0249 (fax)

Canadian Restaurant & Foodservice Association
316 Bloor Street West
Toronto, Ontario Canada
M5S1W5
(416)923-8416
(416)923-1450 (fax)

Ontario Restaurant Association
121 Richmond Street West, Suite 1201
Toronto, Ontario Canada
M6S2P2
(416)359-0533
(416)359-0531 (fax)

**Virgin Islands Restaurant &
Bar Association**
c/o Virgin Rhythms Public
    Relations
P.O. Box 12048
St. Thomas, VI 00801
(809)777-9440
(809)779-7716 (fax)

APPENDIX
E

Code of Professional Standards for the Practice of Public Relations: Public Relations Society of America

---

This code was adopted by the PRSA Assembly in 1988. It replaces a Code of Ethics in force since 1950 and revised in 1954, 1959, 1963, 1977, and 1983.

DECLARATION OF PRINCIPLES

Members of the Public Relations Society of America base their professional principles on the fundamental value of dignity of the individual, holding that the free exercise of human rights, especially freedom of speech, freedom of assembly, and freedom of the press, is essential to the practice of public relations.

In serving the interests of clients and employers, we dedicate ourselves to the goals of better communication, understanding, and cooperation among the diverse individuals, groups, and institutions of society, and of equal opportunity of employment in the public relations profession.

We pledge:
To conduct ourselves professionally, with truth, accuracy, fairness, and responsibility to the public;
To improve our individual competence and advance the knowledge and proficiency of the profession through continuing research and education;
And to adhere to the articles of the Code of Professional Standards for the Practice of Public Relations as adopted by the governing assembly of the society.

CODE OF PROFESSIONAL STANDARDS FOR THE PRACTICE OF PUBLIC RELATIONS

The articles have been adopted by the Public Relations Society of America to promote and maintain high standards of public service and ethical conduct among its members.

1. A member shall conduct his or her professional life in accord with the **public interest.**
2. A member shall exemplify high standards of **honesty and integrity** while carrying out dual obligations to a client or employer and to the democratic process.
3. A member shall **deal fairly** with the public, with past or present clients or employers, and with fellow practitioners, giving due respect to the ideal of free inquiry and to the opinions of others.
4. A member shall adhere to the highest standards of **accuracy and truth,** avoiding extravagant claims or unfair comparisons and giving credit for ideas and words borrowed from others.
5. A member shall not knowingly disseminate **false or misleading information** and shall act promptly to correct erroneous communications for which he or she is responsible.
6. A member shall not engage in any practice which has the purpose of **corrupting** the integrity of channels of communications or the processes of government.
7. A member shall be prepared to **identify publicly** the name of the client or employer on whose behalf any public communication is made.
8. A member shall not use any individual or organization professing to serve or represent an announced cause, or professing to be independent or unbiased, but actually serving another or **undisclosed interest.**

9. A member shall not **guarantee the achievement** of specified results beyond the member's direct control.

10. A member shall **not represent conflicting** or competing interests without the express consent of those concerned, given after a full disclosure of the facts.

11. A member shall not place himself or herself in a position where the member's **personal interest is or may be in conflict** with an obligation to an employer or client, or others, without full disclosure of such interests to all involved.

12. A member shall **not accept fees, commissions, gifts or any other consideration** from anyone except clients or employers for whom services are performed without their express consent, given after full disclosure of the facts.

13. A member shall scrupulously safeguard the **confidences and privacy rights** of present, former, and prospective clients or employers.

14. A member shall not intentionally **damage the professional reputation** or practice of another practitioner.

15. If a member has evidence that another member has been guilty of unethical, illegal, or unfair practices, including those in violation of this Code, the member is obligated to present the information promptly to the proper authorities of the Society for action in accordance with the procedure set forth in Article XII of the Bylaws.

16. A member called as a witness in a proceeding for enforcement of this Code is obligated to appear, unless excused for sufficient reason by the judicial panel.

17. A member shall, as soon as possible, sever relations with any organization or individual if such relationship requires conduct contrary to the articles of this Code.

Reprinted with persmission by Public Relations Society of America, 33 Irving Place, New York, NY 10003-2376, Tel. 212-995-2230.

Travel Industry Organizations

Travel Industry Association of America
1100 New York Avenue, NW
Suite 450
Washington, DC 20005-3934
202-408-8422

Travel & Tourism Research Association
10200 West 44th Avenue
Wheat Ridge, CO 80033
303-940-6557

U.S. Travel Data Center
1100 New York Avenue, NW
Suite 450
Washington, DC 20005-3934
202-408-8422

Suggested References

Albrecht, Karl. *The Only Thing That Matters: Bringing Power by the Customer into the Center of Your Business.* Harper Business, New York, 1992.

Baker, Kim, and Baker, Sunny. *How to Promote, Publicize & Advertise Your Growing Business: Getting the Word Out Without Spending a Fortune.* John Wiley, New York, 1992.

Bernays, Edward L. *The Engineering of Consent.* The University of Oklahoma, Norman, OK, 1955.

Bernays, Edward L. *Crystallizing Public Opinion.* Liveright Publishing Company, New York, 1961.

Bernstein, Alan B. *Emergency Public Relations Manual.* Pase, Highland Park, NJ, 1988.

Black, Sam, and Sharpe, Melvin A. *Practice Public Relations: Common Sense Guidelines for Business and Professional People.* Prentice-Hall, Englewood Cliffs, NJ, 1983.

Bly, Robert W. *Targeted Public Relations: How to Get Thousands of Dollars of Free Publicity for Your Product, Service Organization or Idea.* H. Holt, New York, 1993.

Budd, John F., Jr. *Street Smart Public Relations: A Top Pro Tells How to Get Things Done.* Turtle Publications, Evanston, IL, 1992.

Cutlip, Scott, Center, Allen H., and Broom, Glen M. *Effective Public Relations.* Prentice-Hall, Englewood Cliffs, NJ, 1985.

Darrow, Richard W., Forrestal, Dan J., and Cookman, Aubrey O. *Public Relations Handbook.* Dartnell Corporation, Chicago, 1968.

Desanick, Robert C. *Managing to Keep the Customer: How to Achieve and Maintain Superior Customer Service throughout the Organization.* Jossey-Bass, San Francisco, 1987.

Dilenschneider, Robert L. *Power and Influence: Mastering the Art of Persuasion.* Prentice-Hall, Englewood Cliffs, NJ, 1990.

Dwyer, Thomas W. *Simply Public Relations: Public Relations Made Challenging, Complete & Concise!* New Forums, Stillwater, OK, 1992.

Goldman, Gordon. *Public Relations in the Marketing Mix: Introducing Vulnerability Relations.* Crain Books, Chicago, 1984.

Gottschalk, Jack A. *Crisis Response: Inside Stories on Managing Image Under Siege.* Southwestern College Publishing, Cincinnati, 1993.

Harris, Thomas L. *Marketer's Guide to Public Relations.* John Wiley, New York, 1991.

Hausman, Carl, and Benoit, Philip. *Positive Public Relations.* Liberty House-Tab Books, Blue Ridge Summit, PA, 1989.

Levine, Michael. *Guerilla P.R.: How to Wage an Effective Publicity Campaign—Without Going Broke.* Harper Business, New York, 1993.

Lewes, Herschell Gordon. *How to Handle Your Own Public Relations.* Nelson-Hall, Chicago, 1977.

Lewis, H. G. *How to Handle Your Own Public Relations.* Nelson-Hall, Chicago, 1976.

Lewis, Robert C., and Chambers, Richard E. *Marketing Leadership in Hospitality.* Van Nostrand Reinhold, New York, 1989.

Lovelock, Christopher. *Services Marketing.* Prentice-Hall, Englewood Cliffs, NJ, 1991.

Martin, Dick. *The Executive's Guide to Handling a Press Interview.* Pilot Books, Babylon, NY, 1994.

Moore, H. Frazier, and Canfield, Berthrand R. *Public Relations Principles, Cases and Problems.* Richard D. Irwin, Homewood, IL, 1977.

Newsom, Doug, and Carrell, Bob. *Public Relations Writing: Form & Style.* Wadsworth, Belmont, CA, 1991.

Newsom, Doug, Scott, Alan, and Turk, Judy Van Slyke. *The Realities of Public Relations.* Wadsworth, Belmont, CA, 1993.

Nolte, Lawrence W. *Fundamentals of Public Relations: Professional Guidelines, Concepts and Integrations.* Pergamon Press, New York, 1979.

Nykiel, Ronald A. *Keeping Customers in Good Times and Bad.* Berkley Books, New York, 1992.

Ramacitti, David F. *Do-It-Yourself Publicity.* Amacom/American Management Association, New York, 1991.

Reilly, Robert T. *Public Relations in Action.* Prentice-Hall, Englewood Cliffs, NJ, 1981.

Seitel, Fraser P. *The Practice of Public Relations.* Merrill Publishing Macmillan, Columbus, OH, 1989.

Swift, Paul, ed. Edward L. Bernays, *The Later Years: Public Relations Insights, 1956–1986.* H&M Publishers, Rhinebeck, NY, 1989.

Wragg, David. *Targeting Media Relations: A Step-by-Step Guide to Cost-Effective Public Relations.* Kogan Page Educ.-Taylor & Francis, Bristol, PA, 1994.

Index